Agriculture Heritage

Agriculture Heritage

V. Radha Krishna Murthy
Ph.D., PGDES
Professor and Head
Department of Agronomy
ANGRAU, Agricultural College,
Bapatla, A.P. 522101

M. Sree Rekha
M.Sc (Ag) Ph.D
Associate Professor
Department of Agronomy
ANGRAU, Agricultural College,
Bapatla, A.P. 522101

BSP **BS Publications**
A unit of **BSP Books Pvt. Ltd.**
4-4-309/316, Giriraj Lane, Sultan Bazar,
Hyderabad - 500 095.

Agriculture Heritage by V. Radha Krishna Murthy and M. Sree Rekha

Published by:

BS Publications
A unit of **BSP Books Pvt., Ltd.**

4-4-309/316, Giriraj Lane, Sultan Bazar,
Hyderabad - 500 095
Phone : 040 - 23445688, 23445600
e-mail : info@bspbooks.net
www.bspbooks.net

Printed at
Aditya Offset Process (I) Pvt. Ltd.
Hyderabad.

Price: Rs. 100.00
ISBN: 9789386819451

Dedicated to

Lord Tirumala Tirupati
Sri Venkateswara Swami Vaariki

ASIAN AGRI-HISTORY FOUNDATION
(AAHF)

2 September 2017

Tel. +91 (294) 2460221
E-mail:
asianagrihistory94@gmail.com
yeshwantn2@gmail.com

***OLD ADDRESS*:**
47 ICRISAT Colony-1,
Brig. Sayeed Road
Secunderabad 500009 TS

NEW ADDRESS
105, Vidhya Nagar, Hiran magri,
Sector.4, Udaipur 313 002

Foreword

Ever since the British introduced teaching agriculture in Indian institutions from the 19th century CE, the Course content entirely followed the European knowledge base. Traditional knowledge of agriculture developed over several millennia in India was downplayed as outdated. For the last one century, Indian agricultural knowledge base has been built upon the European and American agriculture. This has done unmeasurable harm to the growth of our agriculture. It is imperative to expedite resurrection of our agricultural knowledge based on wisdom and experience of our ancestors.

The Asian Agri-History Foundation, since 1997, has been requesting the Indian Council of Agricultural Research (ICAR) to introduce course or courses on Indian agricultural heritage in the curriculum of agricultural colleges all over the country. The trustees of the Asian Agri-History Foundation would like to place on record utmost gratitude to ICAR for introducing agricultural heritage course in the undergraduate curriculum of agricultural colleges of India. In the last 20 years, a great deal of documented knowledge of agriculture, animal husbandry, and commodity trade has been found and printed. Books written agricultural heritage are now available for teachers and students.

I have noted with great happiness the hard work put in recently by Dr. V.R.K. Murthy and Dr. M. Sree Rekha in writing this textbook on agricultural heritage based on the syllabus suggested by the ICAR. The contents of the manuscript have impressed me immensely. Teaching with books available on agricultural heritage would stimulate students to dig ancient manuscripts that are still hidden. In addition, the young minds will start acknowledging and admiring the wisdom of our farmer-ancestors. Our current and future research work should be based on our own agricultural heritage, utilizing modern techniques.

Let the young agriculturist contribute to making India a superpower in Food production and security in the near future. God will surely bless them.

[Y L Nene]
Emeritus Chairman
Asian Agri-History Foundation

Please visit our website: www.asianagrihistory.org

Contents

Chapter 3

Soil and Water Management

Chapter 4

Plant Protection and ITKs

Chapter 5

Medicinal Plants and Seed Health

Chapter 6

Civilization- Journey in Agriculture

Chapter 1

The Genesis of Agriculture

"We are all born with a divine fire in us. Our effort should be to give wings to this fire" ***- Dr. A. P. J Abdul Kalam***

1.1 Introduction to Indian Agriculture Heritage

Definition: Agriculture heritage is defined as "The techniques and ways of growing crops and rearing animals which are constantly adapted to time, place and local culture that are handed over as a tradition".

Human being (*Homo sapiens*) has been on the earth for approximately 2 million years. He has been a hunter gatherer for 99.5 per cent of existence and this period is considered as the most successful. Only, 12,000 years ago he started domesticating plants and recognized weather as the most precious natural resource. He managed environments in which he lived for generations by following environmental friendly agricultural practices and without significantly damaging local ecologies. This indicates that ancient knowledge has immense potential to manage the risks in agriculture. However, in the past 200 years of scientific agriculture there has been an over exploitation of natural resources and the environment has degraded.

History unveils that the genesis of agriculture in India as a means of sustaining human life can be traced back to 10,000 BC or 12,000 years ago. However, in the absence of written records about the beginning of agriculture in the pre historic India, one has to depend on archeo-botanical materials obtained during several archaeological excavations conducted in India.

In ancient times India was primarily referred to by two names *viz.*, (a) Bharatvarsh and (b) Jambudweep. To the west of India is the land of "pariha", which evolved into modern Iran. The history of agriculture and civilization go hand in hand as the food production made it possible for primitive man to settle down in areas leading to formation of society and initiation of civilization. The development of civilization and agriculture had passed through several stages (ages).

1.2 Stages / Ages

Archaeologists initially classified the stages (ages) as (a) stone age (b) bronze age and (c) iron age.

(a) ***Stone age:*** The scholars split up the stone age into (i) *Paleolithic age (old stone age) (ii) Mesolithic age (new stone age) (iii) Neolithic age*

- *Paleolithic age (old stone age):* This period is characterized by the food gatherers and hunters. The man started making stone tools, choppers and rude choppers
- *Mesolithic age (new stone age):* The transitional period between the end of paleolithic age and beginning of neolithic age is called mesolithic age. It began about 10,000 BC and ended with the rise of agriculture (7500 BC to 6500 BC). This period is characterized by stone implements called microliths. People lived as food gatherers and hunters. The domestication of animals was the major achievement of the mesolithic age hunter
- *Neolithic age:* This age is also known as agricultural revolution age (7500 BC to 6500 BC), because during this period discovery of agriculture took place in western Asia (Israel, Jordan, Iran etc). In this region wild ancestors of two cereals wheat and barley and of domesticated animals like goat, sheep, pig and cattle were found. Polished stone axe and sickle were used for cultivation of crops like wheat, barley, rice, maize and millets. Horse and ass were used as draught and transport animals. The distinguishing feature of this age is that the farmers built their houses with locally available material. Pots for storing of food grain and weaving with wool are other developments. This age brought major changes in techniques of food production which gave the farmer control over his environment and saved him from the precarious existence of mere hunter and gatherer of wild berries and roots
- The main features of neolithic culture in India
  - economic and technological development

- use of polished stone axes for clearing and cleaning bushes
- handmade pottery for storing food grains
- invention of textile weaving
- the discovery of silk
- cultivation of rice, banana sequence and yam in eastern part of India
- cultivation of millets and pulses in South India.

(b) ***Bronze age** (Chalcolithic culture 3000-1700 BC):* In this age, stone implements along with copper and bronze were used. The chalcolithic revolution began in Mesopotamia and spread to Egypt and Indus valley. The significant features are (a) invention of plough (b) shifting of agriculture from hilly areas to lower river valley areas (c) flood water were stored for irrigation and canals were dug (d) sowing of seed by dibbling with a pointed stick.

(c) ***Iron age:*** The Aryans knew the use of iron. India entered iron age during Vedic period. When Rigveda was composed the iron age already commenced. Farmers used iron for making implements.

1.3 Periods

The periods in agricultural heritage are A. Ancient period B. Medieval period and C. Modern period

A. ***Ancient period:***10,000 BC to beginning of Anno Domini (AD)

B. ***Medieval period:*** beginning of AD to 18th Century

C. ***Modern period:*** 19th Century to date

1.4 The Genesis of Agriculture and its Chronological Arrangement

A comprehensive account of ancient agricultural practices, from prehistory to 1200 AD, is given in "Agriculture in ancient India-a report" written by S P Raychaudhuri and Mira Roy, published by the Indian Council of Agricultural Research (ICAR) in 1993. This report uses the following chronological arrangement:

(A) Prehistory: (6600 BC-1000 BC)

(B) Protohistory: Chalcolithic and iron age (2320 BC-450 BC)

(C) Historic period: (500 BC-1200 AD)

- Early historic period (500 BC-100 BC)
- Mid historic period (start of the Christian era-1200 AD).

A. 12000 to 9500 years ago

- Hunters and food gatherers stage existed
- Stone implements were seen throughout the Indian subcontinent
- Tribals of Madhya Pradesh (Bastar, Betul, Chhindwara, Jhabua) have never experienced famine. However, if experienced they ate 165 edible tree products, shrubs, and climbers; seeds of 31 plants were roasted for eating; roots/tubers of 19 plants were eaten after roasting/boiling. Honey was used for sugar
- Earliest agriculture was by vegetative propagation (e.g., bananas, sugarcane, yam, palms and ginger)

B. 9500 to 7500 years ago

- Neolithic agricultural revolution occurred in western Asia (9500-8500 years ago) mainly in the "fertile crescent" (hilly regions embracing Israel, Jordon, Anatolia in Turkey, Iran, Caspian basin, and adjoining Iranian plateau)
- In the "fertile crescent", wild ancestors of wheat and barley, goat, sheep, pig and cattle were found

C. 7500 to 5000 years ago

- Significant features were invention of plough, irrigated farming, use of wheel, and metallurgy and in Egypt seed dibbling
- Rigveda was composed 5700 years ago. Agriculture was well developed
- Earliest record of rice was from Non Nok Tha in Thailand, 5500 years ago

D. 5000 to 4000 years ago

- Harappan culture existed in India
- Excavations in Kalibangan (western Rajasthan) revealed ploughed field. Mostly post rainy season crops were grown
- Early evidence of a seed drill has been found in Lothal
- Wheeled carts were commonly used in the Indus valley
- Bullock carts from Lothal had solid wheels

- River boats were used for carrying grain. Agriculture, fishing and trade were the main occupations
- Gram (chickpea) remains have been found in Kalibangan; sesame which originated in west Africa was brought to India directly or via Mesopotamia; later, sesame was taken from India to China

E. 4000 to 2000 years ago

- Original focus of settlements in south India was Raichur/Bellary
- There is a record of sorghum grain from Inamgaon, Maharashtra
- Fingermillet found at Hallur dated 1800 BC
- Also minor millets, *Setaria* and *Panicum* were eaten
- In Inamgaon (Maharashtra), people cultivated wheat, *kulthi*, mung bean, and pea. Channels from the river were made for irrigation
- In eastern India, rice, bananas, and sugarcane were cultivated
- Excavations at Pandu, Rejar, and Dhibi in West Bengal revealed that rice, fish, meat of neelgai, deer and pig were consumed as food

F. The Vedic, Buddhist, and Jain Age

- Carpenters made ploughs, chariots and doors. Aryans used copper and leather
- Ploughing was mentioned frequently in Rigveda
- Irrigation was practiced from rivers. Wells were also used
- Farm land was measured
- The harvesting tool was sickle
- Rice was cultivated
- Benefits of crop rotation were appreciated
- Plant protection against moles, birds, and "blight" has been mentioned in Atharvanaveda
- Krishi-Parashara was written around 400 BC, in Takshsila-Sialkot region
- Artha Shastra (400 BC) and the Pali texts, Mahavagya and Kallavagya (300 BC) were sources of information on agriculture

- Artha Shastra mentions river beds for cultivation of cucurbits, and planting in furrows between two rows of Vetiver. Crops mentioned are
    - rice, sesame during the beginning of rainy season
    - *mung* and blackgram during mid-rainy season
    - safflower, lentil, horsegram, barley, wheat, pea, chickpea, linseed, mustard during end of post rainy season
    - seed treatments were recommended to ensure good germination
    - sugarcane cut ends were plastered with honey, ghee, and cow dung
    - cotton seeds were treated with cow dung
    - sprouts of seeds were manured with a fresh haul of minute fishes and irrigated with milk of *snuhi.*

G. Emperor Ashoka (274-237 BC)

- Emperor Ashoka prohibited burning of forests
- He promoted and adopted a state policy on arboriculture and horticulture–first ever in the world
- He built houses in every 9 miles for men/animals to take rest
- He encouraged planting of mango, banana, grapevine, jack fruit, palm and wild datepalm.

H. Satavahanas (Andhras) (100 BC-200 AD)

- The Satavahanas ruled Andhra, Karnataka, Vidarbha, Malwa, and western Rajasthan
- Coconut was propagated first on the east coast during this period. The Satavahana king, Nahapana, gifted large coconut plantations to people
- Takshasila became a centre for development of iron technology and iron was exported to west Asia
- The variety of farm implements increased
- Cultivation of rice, fingermillet, sugarcane, cotton, pepper, and turmeric was common. Tank irrigation was developed and practiced widely. In drylands *ragi* and other minor millets were planted

- Varahamihira (astrologer, astronomer, encyclopedist) wrote Brihat Samhita (agriculture, plant protection, and manuring)
- Amarkosha written by Amar Simha contains information on soil, irrigation and agricultural implements; describes 12 types of land
- ***1500-1000 years ago***
- Information on agriculture was based on the book of Hiuen Tsang (Chinese scholar) and in Harshacharita, written by Banabhatta
- Fertile soils of Magadh and Malwa were productive and suitable for wheat in winter
- Cereals such as wheat, rice, millets, and fruits were extensively grown. A 60-day variety and fragrant varieties of rice were mentioned
- Arecanut, nutmeg, and camphor oil were mentioned
- Ginger, mustard, melons, pumpkin, onion and garlic were also mentioned.

1.5 Homes of Evolution of Agriculture "Old and New" World

Researchers have identified seven (7) homes of evolution of agriculture in the "old" world and three (3) in the "new" world.

A. In the "old" world

- Oldest center of diversity and origin of cultivated species of plants in southeast Asia comprising Thailand, Malaysia and adjoining areas for rice, sugarcane, banana, coconut, cardamoms and turmeric
- Second oldest center was the "fertile crescent" in west Asia for wheat, forages, olive, grapes and almond
- Third was south India for rice, jute, *desi* cotton, pulses, mango, citrus species and black pepper
- Fourth was China for soybean, apricot, litchi and some citrus species
- Fifth was northern India, Afghanistan and Iran for bread wheat, rye, linseed and walnut
- Sixth was the center bordering the Mediterranean for oats, temperate zone fruits, vegetables, cabbage and cauliflower

- Seventh was Ethiopia for wheat, sorghum, castor, barley, coffee and watermelon.

B. ***In the "new" world***

- Mexico for maize, sweet potato, cotton, chillies, guava, pumpkin, and beans
- Peru and Bolivia for potato, tomato, and tobacco
- Argentina and Brazil for rubber, cashewnut, cocoa, groundnut and pineapple.

1.6 Early Indigenous and Other Domesticated Crops

Besides rice, the indigenous people of India domesticated minor millets, grain legumes, oilseeds and other crops.

A. Southwest Asian domesticates

Several species of winter cereals (wheat, barley), legumes and other crops were domesticated in southwest Asia and several of those crops diffused into India.

B. African domesticates

Sorghum, fingermillet and pearlmillet were domesticated in Africa. These crops diffused into India around 2000 BC, and were identified from several archaeological sites.

Chapter 2

Farmers in Ancient Society

"The more decisions you can make avoiding external pressures which will constantly try to manipulate and immobilize you, the better your life will be. The entire nation will benefit by having strong inner directed people as its citizens" ***- Dr. A. P. J Abdul Kalam***

2.1 Status of Farmers in Ancient Society

- The early human civilizations viz., Egyptian, Mesopotamian, and Indus valley civilizations developed in river valleys lying upto about 35^0 North latitude
- During Neolithic period, human settlements were established with the initiation of domestication of animals and plants and deviation from pastoral life
- Man began to use polished stoneware
- The early home of Aryans was in south Russia in the steppes between the Danube, the Volga and the Urals
- The Vedic Aryan farmers had large forests at their disposal for securing timber, plants, herbs and medicinal plants
- In social rank Aryan farmers were considered high and the entire village administration was in the hands of farmers known as "kutumbins"
- In the Chalcolithic period, Harappan farmers had reached a high state of culture

- Harappans cultivated wheat, barley, sesame, pea, melon, datepalm and *Brassica* spp. Cotton was an important crop, the centre of its origin being the Indus Valley
- Harappan culture covered a vast area in north India with very strong settlements at various sites in Jammu and Kashmir, Punjab, Haryana, Rajasthan, Gujarat, Uttar Pradesh, and Madhya Pradesh
- One of the most important findings has been that the inhabitants of Ahar, a Harappan site in Udaipur ate rice
- This rice had long seeded grain and was the ancestor of the fragrant basmati rice
- Wheat and *jowar* were the other food crops
- Farmers possessed expert skills in raising crops and fruit trees
- Farmers paid 1/6th to 1/12th of their produce or products to the ruler
- Early Vedic Aryans were primarily pastoral. When they settled in Punjab they cut jungles, built their villages, grazed their cattle in jungles, and planted barley in the land close to their habitation.

2.2 Status of Women

The norms set by tradition regarding food, food consumption, food distribution and other related issues were all intended to ensure proper utilization of food and contributed a great deal to preventing scarcity of food. Women played a major role in the practical application of these traditional norms and have contributed considerably in providing food security for families and for society.

A. Role of women in agriculture

- In Vedic period the economy of people was largely dependent on agriculture along with cattle rearing, in which women performed highly respectable activities
- Women took part in agricultural activities like ploughing, sowing, weeding, harvesting, threshing etc.
- Women also assisted husband and grown up children and performed hard agricultural duties and brought glory to their home thereby to the village and country

- During Vedic period besides agricultural activities women involved in subsidiary activities like cloth making, weaving, spinning and dyeing
- There was also mention of women involved in carpentry, ornaments making, military training etc.
- During Vedic period women contributed a lot to build the economy not only of their own families but also of the country too.

B. *Women in highly respectable formal manner*

- The custom of the bride carrying with her a small idol of goddess Annapurna is observed to this day in several communities and families. Annapurna, as the name suggests, is one who assures food supply all the time and is another form of the Goddess Parvati
- Another custom – again observed to this day – is that of the new bride spilling a tumbler full of food grains with a push of her foot when she enters her husband's house for the first time. This is also symbolic of the women's most respected role in assuring plenty of food grains in that house.

C. *Some excerpts of conversation among mothers in the family*

The following excerpts of conversations were found in the ancient times:

- "I concealed away some food grains for emergency"
- "I carefully kept aside food for the supplicants"
- "I prepared special dishes on festive occasions"
- "I served special food to honored guests of the household"
- "Thousands of students on completion of their education and ascetics daily frequented our home. Honored them all by offering clothes, food, etc. Thousands of maids served plateful of food every day"
- "I looked after the accounts of the home. I saw to it that the treasuries were always full like an ocean."

D. *Other most respected responsibilities of mothers*

- In addition to taking care of children and other household work, the village housewife actively participated in the farming activities
- Village women, in addition to cooking food had to carry the meals to the family members working in the fields'

- When the farmer performed formal ceremonies of agriculture, the housewife was given equal importance as men and allowed to officially participate in the ceremonies
- Poor women forgot their poverty at the sight of a rich yield
- Food was never supposed to be exhausted. If it was, due to poverty, poor village women protected the family honour equally with men by working very hard
- Food management of the family was a challenging and most respected responsibility for the housewife
- She is goddess Lakshmi herself residing in the house
- Maximum utilization of food stocks without wastage was clearly managed by the housewife
- The poor housewife fed her young children and offered the remaining food to the neighbor who was poorer than her, herself going without food.

Literature holds a mirror to life. These illustrations, therefore, show how food management within the family and through it the very honour of the family, rested with the crowned queen of both the rich and the poor households of ancient India. It also shows that the traditional values regarding food and its distribution and consumption at the family level were successfully managed by the housewives. They have thus played a very significant role in ensuring food security for the nation, equally and more than men.

2.3 Advice by Sages to Kings on their Duties towards Farmers

Advice given by the sages in the past has withstood the tides of time and has definite relevance even today.

- Sage Parashara advised "May the farmers be happy, healthy and wealthy"
- Another sage Kashyapa considered agriculture "a noble profession"
- Sages and scholars advised kings to ensure that farmers were contended and comfortable

B. Summer Ploughing

- Summer ploughing is another cultural practice invari followed. This is now known to expose resting spores of soil borne plant pathogens (such as *Sclerotium rolfsii*) to solar radiation leading to reduction of their inoculum. In Rajasthan, this practice hastened rapid decay of onion debris containing *Alternaria porri* and consequently reduced the inoculum level in the soil.

C. Stubble burning

- After harvest of rice crop, the stubbles are burnt before preparing the field for the next crop. This practice reduced the inoculum of *Leptosphaeria sahrnii* and hence stem rot incidence in subsequent rice crop was drastically reduced.

D. Rice – Banana Rotation

- Rotation of rice with banana help to reduce the inoculum of *Fusarium oxysporum* causing Panama wilt of banana. It has been found that under water stagnated conditions in rice fields, the population of the pathogen is reduced below the minimum threshold.

E. Mixed cropping

- Mixed cropping help to reduce airborne fungal diseases as well as vector borne viral diseases. When one short crop chilli is grown with a tall crop like sorghum, the aphid vectors carrying the stylet borne viruses (potato virus), first alight on the tall crop and make a few feeding probes to find out its suitability as food. In this process the virus present in their stylets is lost. Consequently, when they move to chilli, they have very little virus in their stylets and hence the virus transmission is greatly reduced. Tall crops also act as wind barriers affecting the free movement of wind borne spores of several foliar diseases. Thus, spread of foliar fungal diseases is greatly controlled.

F. Pits with straw lining

- Several ingenious practices of storage of vegetables and grains are in vogue from ancient times. Winter vegetables were preserved for use in summer in pits lined with wheat straw spread on all four sides, bottom, and top and covered with soil. This insulated the vegetables against summer heat and maintained them under cool conditions. Consequently, microbial spoilage of the vegetables was greatly reduced.

G. Neem tree and products

➢ *Neem leaves*

- For grain storage, neem leaves have been spread over rice bags traditionally to protect against storage pests. The storage pests from nearby fields and old stores settle on new leaves and lay eggs on the leaf surface. Agricultural chemists have identified several chemicals such as nimbeen and *azadirachtin* act as repellents to these storage pests. *Azadirachtin* has been found to have anti-feedant and repellent properties to more than 200 pests. It is able to arrest growth of pests, reduce their fecundity, and hatching of their eggs, but does not affect their natural enemies. In ancient period without chemical pesticides, neem leaves effectively served the purpose
- Another scientific effect of spreading neem leaves over groundnut in storage is that neem leaves inhibit the growth of *Aspergillus flavus* and thereby prevent aflatoxin production.

➢ *Neem cake*

- Neem cake application to the field was an ancient technic. The modern agriculture proved to reduce population of soil borne fungal and nematode pathogens. Calcium and Magnesium present in neem cake helps to reclaim alkaline soils.

➢ *Neem tree*

- Ancient farmers grew 1-2 neem trees for one hectare of land and in and around their houses. The modern agriculture found neem tree to be an effective air filter and protects the environment. The leaf area of 1 m^2 absorbs 2.88 g dust. At the same time, neem tree is not sensitive to toxic chemicals. This has been proved in the "Bhopal tragedy" of 1984 caused by leakage of methyl isocyanate. However, crops such as mustard, radish, and fenugreek were totally destroyed upto 2 km from the factories, the neem trees in this zone exhibited only partial drying of leaves. The trunk and branches were not killed. The trees rejuvenated next spring. The dried leaves contained no residue of the pesticide.

H. *Grain storage*

- The first known method of grain storage practiced by man was in underground pits for storage of large quantities of grain. Scientifically this can be explained on the basis of depletion of oxygen and increase in carbondioxide. These conditions are adverse for survival of storage pests. Today in controlled atmosphere storage, hermetically sealed bins are used to replace oxygen by carbondioxide which causes anoxia and kills insects
- Small quantities of grains are stored in earthen vessels in houses and closed with lids. These vessels are painted with castor oil which is now known to be a barrier to moisture ingress.

I. *Seed processing*

- Seeds are treated with coal ash before storage. By this age old practice, larvae and adults of storage pests that attack the grain at the time of storage are killed. Coal ash absorbs moisture from the seeds and thereby kills the pests already inside the grain. Now-a-days activated clay is used for the same purpose. It was invented in 1640 AD to preserve cereals by causing lethal dehydration of storage pests and thereby overcome food shortage in famine years. Egyptians are well known for their knowledge of storage of not only grains but also mummies inside the pyramids. The bodies of their rulers have not decomposed even after 5000 years
- Pigeonpea seeds are coated with red earth before storage. The notorious pulse beetle lays eggs in mature grains in the field. The harvested grains contain the grubs inside. The red earth coating prevents the emergence of adults from such grains. The insects die inside the grains and thus the infestation does not spread
- The simple method of sun drying of grains before storage reduces the moisture content. It has been found that storage insects cannot thrive in grains with less than 10% moisture. Further, the source of infestation, *i.e.,* eggs and larvae on the harvested grains, are killed while sun drying when the temperature reaches 40°C.

J. *Other Practices*

- Our ancestors also were well versed in horticulture as seen from *Sthalavriksha* of Ekambarnath temple in Kancheepuram, Tamil

Nadu. Four branches of a mango tree in the temple bear fruits of four varieties of mangoes. The tree must have been produced by inarching four seedlings of four varieties so that the trunk is united while the branches bear fruits of the concerned variety

- Another important innovation of our ancestors is lime. When the mortar of 1000 year old temple towers was chemically analyzed it was found to contain copper sulphide in addition to lime. This indicates that the mold inhibiting power of a mixture of copper sulphate and lime was known to our people 1000 years ago. We now know the anti fungal properties of Bordeaux mixture for which the French chemist Millardet was given the credit in 1884.

Chapter 3

Soil and Water Management

"Your willingness to use your own inner resources, especially your imagination, will bring you success. When you undertake a task from your own uniquely individual stand point, you will become a person"

- Dr. A. P. J Abdul Kalam

3.0 Soil Management

3.1 Soil Definition and Concept

During the Vedic period farmers believed that if they prayed to the forces of nature which are Gods, that were unknown and unexplained they are protected and their agriculture flourishes. These are sky, soil, wind, fire and water. Among these the farmers relied to the highest level on the blessings of "mother earth" "bhoomata" and worshipped as Goddess. The mother earth (soil) is the only most pious and most revered planet known to support "life" so far, is worshipped also as "prithvi". Sky is considered to be the "father" who is the chief of the deities, hence the name "father sky" or "pitaa".

Depending upon the purpose and perception, the word "soil" has different meanings for different people. In the Oxford Dictionary, "soil" as a noun connotes the upper layer of the earth in which plants grow. In reverence for this natural resource and to make the term convey dynamism, "soil" is considered as "soul of infinite life." In Indian native perception, soil is considered as the "origin of life". From the point of view of agricultural use, soil is the loose earth surface that supports vegetation, its quality determining the type and density of vegetation. Farmers through the ages have treated soil as a "living entity".

Soil serves six functions : (i) produces biomass (ii) performs filtering, buffering, and transformation reactions (iii) a source of biodiversity (iv) supports infrastructural development (roads, railways, waterways, homestead/farmstead) (v) supplies geogenic/pedogenic raw materials and (vi) preserve cultural heritages of landform/soilscape.

3.2 Historical Background

- Since times immemorial, soil has been regarded as nourishing all animates, moving and static
- It was written in a 1500 year old Sanskrit text that "upon this handful of soil our survival depends. Husband it and it will grow our food, our field and our shelter and surround us with beauty. Otherwise, the soil will collapse"
- *Jhum* cultivation is defined as "slash and burning of existing vegetation to gain soil for agriculture and after two or three cropping cycles leave it for regeneration of original vegetation". It is a typical example of the faith which signifies a fit between man's needs and soil's health
- The ancient treatment of soils in India describes it (synonymous with earth and land) as one of the five elements of life, the other four being sky, wind, fire and water. In telugu soil has been described as the "mother" and all living beings as her "children"
- The Mother Earth, referred to as "soil" is rich in energy
- In his treatise on agriculture, *Kashyapiya krishisukti*, Kashyapa pointed out that a good soil should have substantial mass and be devoid of bones and stones; plastic clay with reddish and black hue; not too deep or shallow; conducive to speedy seedling emergence; easy for ploughing and other operations; and capable of easily absorbing moisture and being inhabited by beneficial living creatures
- Inconsistent ability of diverse soils to sustain plant growth and yields is found in a Biblical arable, which states, "Once there was a man who went out to sow some corn. As he broadcast the seeds in the field, some of it fell along the path and the birds came and ate it up. Some of it fell on the rocky ground where there was little soil. The seeds soon sprouted because the soil was not deep. But, when the sun came up it burnt the young plants because the

roots have not grown enough, the plants soon dried up. Some of the seed fell among thorny bushes, which grew up and choked the plants. But, some seed fell in the good soil and the plants produced corn; some produced a hundred grains, other thirty and others sixty.

3.3 Ancient and Medieval Systems of Soil Classification

A. Ancient systems of soil classification

- Soil use and color based classification

  In ancient and medieval India, soil was classified based on its color and crop yielding ability. Soil fertility was vital to the concept of soil classification. Atharvanaveda described the color and qualities of earth (soil). The *bhabhru* (soil of brownish colour and of intensive bearing capacity); the *Krishna* (soils of black colour and plowable); and the *rohini* (soils of reddish colour, which enable everything to grow and rise)

- Climate based classification

  Three traditional kinds of soils graded primarily by climate are (i) Jangala (barren) (ii) Anupa (moist) and (iii) Sadharana (ordinary).

B. Medieval Systems of Soil Classification

Medieval systems of classification essentially centered on the following :

- *Economic classification:* based on crop and irrigation. Examples: forest soils, rice soils, irrigated soils
- *Physical classification:* based on texture of soil particles. Examples: khaddar soils, gravelly lands
- *Chemical classification:* based on some chemical properties. Examples: calcareous soils, saline soils, alkaline soils
- *Geological classification:* based primarily on the mode of soil material transport. Examples: alluvial soils (water borne) and Aeolian (wind transported) soils
- *Physiographic classification:* basd mainly on landscape characteristics. Examples: hilly soils, upland soils, lowland soils.

3.4 Ancient and Medieval Systems of Soil Management and its Relevance in Modern day Agriculture

A. Ancient Systems of Soil Management and its relevance in Modern day Agriculture

- Practices of good soil husbandry are as old as the art and science of agriculture itself. In ancient times, when there was more land and less dependent population to support, soil management was based on area extensive practices. Land clearing, shaping, fallowing, shifting cultivation and choice of individual crops and/or their combinations as perceived suitability of soil for different crops were the key strategies of soil management
- What makes a soil richer is, its preparation in a proper way. Only such soils can be called "gold-bearing' or 'gold-crested'
- Since soil was considered one of the five cosmic elements constituting life, its interaction with and interdependence on others for sustaining life was understood and appreciated. The concept known as "holism" recognized that the outcome from the use of soil was influenced by the position and health of the remaining four elements of life. With this perception, ancient man looked for auspicious times of cultivation and seeding of crops to derive maximum benefit from the position of other celestial bodies
- A verse from *Krishi Samgraha* states, that "rain is essential for cultivation and also essential for life. So one should first acquire the knowledge about rainfall"
- The beneficial effect of adding ash to the soil at the conclusion of the "yagna" and its positive influence on crop growth was the starting point supporting use of cattle dung and organic manures. The role and significance of organic matter in soil management was mentioned in the epic *Ramayana*, where it is stated, "all dead things, rotting corpse or stinking garbage, returned to earth are transformed into wholesome things that nourish life". Such is the alchemy of mother earth. In addition to organic farming, use of amendments to restore the quality of acid soils finds mention in a quote by Varro "they manured their fields with a white chalk which they dug out of the field. In addition to soil fertility maintenance, ancient literature also presented a holistic picture on different aspects of soil quality and its management"

- An ancient Tamil saying states, No fodder "No Cow"; No Cow "No manure"; No manure "No crop". Deep in the heart of this ancient knowledge lies the concern for good soil husbandry dependence on use of organic manures and its influence on sustainability of agriculture
- The ancient texts prescribe different decoctions and mixtures for manuring plants. These require the use of animal excreta, fish and fish washings, beef and bone, milk, and extracts of cereals, pulses, green leaves and plants.

B. Medieval Systems of Soil Management and its Relevance in Modern day Agriculture

Like the farmers of ancient times, those of medieval times were aware of the usefulness of organic manures for sustainable crop production.

- Use of cowdung as manure was a common practice
- A 17th century text mentions the use of a wide variety of manures across crops and soils. Crop specific manure combinations and their method of application received particularly elaborate treatment

  Examples: The dung, salt and litter were suggested for soil application in case of palm trees; nectar and vine sap were recommended as foliar application for vines; rotten eggs were considered useful as soil dressing for fig; dung application to soil for olive; pig's dung and human urine as soil application for pomegranate; night soil, animal dung, and sheep's blood for soil application to guava; and cow dung for carrots
- Animal wastes were not the only manures known. There also existed a deep knowledge on the use of green plants and their residues for sustaining soil productivity
- The Holy Quran exhorts farmers to return one-third of the harvest to soils. This commandment signifies sustenance of soil quality through recycling of crop residues. Today we know that ignoring the return of crop residues to soils after harvest is a prime cause of loss of soil quality, falling soil fertility, rising compactability, and spreading erodibility
- Mollison stated that horsegram and sunnhemp had their widespread cultivation to sustain soil fertility, stating, "by the decay of their roots, stems and leaves, make the surface soil much

richer in organic matter, nitrogen, and to a lesser extent in the other elements of nutrition than before their growth". Mollison went on to add that the farmers of medieval India had practical knowledge of the benefits of crop rotations, as they raised mixed crops year after year on the same field

- The Persian manuscript, "*Irshadu Zaraat*", while dealing with the topic of wheat and barley cultivation, mentions that, "grass (residue) on the land may be burned and then the burnt grass may be left on the land as fertilizer"
- The beneficial effects of legumes in maintaining soil fertility were known during the medieval period
- Regular use of organic manures is a guarantee against widening micronutrient deficiencies. Then, besides being a direct source of nutrients, breakdown products of organic manures also influence nutrient availability and produce other non nutrient benefits. Examples: by
  - increasing availability of soil P
  - accelerating availability of Fe and Mn
  - raising availability of micro-nutrients through complexation by organic ligands or decrease in their toxicity
  - reducing loss through ammonia volatilization, leading to increase in fertilizer use efficiency, and
  - buffering of soil pH, improvement in soil structure, buildup of useful soil biology, and increase in soil stability and resilience.

History reveals that civilization began in an environment of irrigation agriculture and the downfall of civilization was determined by water logging and salinity. The inadequate development of irrigation facilities at the project level and poor water management at the farm level have been responsible for large wastage of irrigation water, the low irrigation efficiency, low crop yield, water logging, salinity, alkalinity etc.

3.5 Use of Amendments

Majority of the salt affected soils of India fall in the reclaimable category. The methods of reclamation may, however, vary and may often be location specific depending upon the soil characteristics, climatic conditions and resource availability with the cultivators.

Gypsum is the most common and widely used amendment for the reclamation of alkali soils. Application of gypsum after leaching soluble sulphate if any, and mixing the gypsum upto 10 cm soil depth before the onset of monsoon should be adopted for greater economy and efficiency of reclamation.

Organic acids and carbondioxide released during the course of microbial decomposition of organic amendments and wastes such as molasses and pressmud, besides the native acidity of wastes help to neutralize the alkali and solubilize the free calcium carbonate of alkali soils. Industrial wastes such as phosphogypsum, waste sulphuric acid, spent wash, molasses and pressmud could serve as potential amendments.

3.6 Land Management for Salt Affected Soils

The land management was attended in ancient India as follows:

A. *Land Development*

- Land management for salt affected soils involves clearing unused land to make it fit for cultivation besides providing efficient water management and unrestricted drainage. The field infested with the problem of salinity should be leveled very carefully. In the absence of leveling, the high areas will receive less water and result in little or no leaching as compared to low areas and this will be reflected in patchy growth
- Levelling involves gently grading the land surface along the length to facilitate movement of water in a uniform sheet with desired depth of application.

B. *Piercing*

- In regions such as Bikaner in Rajasthan having relatively less permeable surface layer and highly permeable layer at some depth below, the practice of piercing the impermeable layer has been found to improve leaching of soluble salts. In this practice, 10 cm diameter holes are made with auger to a depth of 3m and these holes are filled up with sand and organic residues. One hundred such holes are sufficient for 1 ha of land which improves leaching efficiency.

C. *Tillage*

- Salts tend to accumulate closer to the soil surface in non irrigated, dry lands and move downward with reclamation and irrigation. Hence, tillage to loosen the dense subsoil prior to irrigation will speed up the movement of soluble salts deeper in the soil upon irrigation

- Deep ploughing and sub soiling improve the physical condition of the soil and loosen the dense subsoil layer and are very effective in alkali soils containing a compact boron horizon which obstructs water percolation and root penetration.

D. *Puddling and Pre plant Submergence*

- Puddling of soil before transplanting of rice is a common practice. The main advantages of this practice are less percolation losses of water and control of weeds. Sodic soils have low permeability and weeds are not a serious problem in such soils. Under such conditions, puddling is a wasteful practice.

E. *Mulching*

- Mulches reduce not only water losses by evaporation but also salt accumulation on the surface of the soil by disrupting capillary continuity.

F. *Fallowing*

- Fallowing encourages the upward movement of saline-sodic groundwater and accumulation of salts on soil surface. Hence, as far as possible, the practice of fallowing should be discouraged.

G. Crop Husbandry

The crop husbandry was practiced as follows:

- *Age of seedling and date of transplanting*

  These two factors determine the final yield of rice crop

- *Planting technique in relation to bed shapes*

  If salinity is a problem, planting seeds in the centre of a single row raised bed will place the seed exactly in the area where salts are expected to concentrate. A double-row raised planting bed by comparison offers an advantage

- *Direction and method of sowing*

  The adverse effect of salinity is minimized by sowing in the northwest slope of ridges

- *Salt tolerant crops*

  Crops such as wheat, barley, cowpea and pearlmillet fail to grow under highly saline conditions. Rice is a well suited crop during reclamation of sodic soils. The high tolerance of rice to alkali conditions is due to its rather superficial root system and its need for a film of water on the soil during its growth.

3.7 Water Management

Successful farming requires careful planning for all farming activities including water resources. The people of ancient times knew that rain was the only source of replenishing water in rivers to provide clean and safe drinking water for them and their domestic animals. They also knew that water was essential for growing food grains from soil and green pastures for their cattle which was their precious wealth. They had a very clear idea about the water cycle and that water on earth evaporates resulting in cloud formation and then comes down again in the form of rain. They also knew that rains last for four months of the year starting after the Sun starts moving southwards (*i.e.,* 22nd June). In Atharvanaveda five sources of water are mentioned. These are: desert (occasional showers), ponds, wells, pits and seasonal rains. Among these, the seasonal rains were the only dependable source for a large area under cultivation.

3.8 Ancient and Prehistoric Methods of Harvesting and Storing of Water

Due to variation in the quantum of rainfall, it was required to store rain water for subsequent use. When the rain water filled the low lying area of land, a lake was formed automatically. Inspired by such a natural phenomenon, ancient people started storing water by making small tanks, ponds and wells.

- Collection and storing surplus water during rainy season and using it during lean season was an important strategy that ancient farmers have used through ages. The practice of collecting water is called "water harvesting". Although the term "water harvesting" is of recent origin, the practice is at least 4000 years old in India, where small tanks and diversion works were used for irrigating the crops
- In Rigveda both kaccha (temporary) and pucca (permanent) wells were mentioned which are the most ancient form of man made storage structure. These wells were used both for drinking purpose and irrigation
- During 700-800 AD much emphasis was given to explore alternative methods of irrigation which included the construction of water

reservoirs. Kashyapa, in his treatise "*Kashyapiya krishisukti*", gave the following details for the construction of water reservoirs

- the water reservoirs should be constructed deep and round, circular or semicircular shape
- the level of ground and direction should be considered
- strong and safe steps should be considered for approaching water
- reservoirs should be equipped with inlets of water and thus be close to a bigger lake situated at higher level or to a mountain spring
- while constructing water reservoir on ground level, it must be ensured that the ground is firm; the reservoir should be big enough to hold abundant water
- safety measures like providing latches should be taken to ward off floods
- these should be regularly examined in rainy season
- *nimba* or neem, kadamba and such other trees should be planted in the vicinity to ensure the purity of water

➢ Apart from the construction of big water reservoirs, Kashyapa also gave instructions regarding digging of wells

➢ In order to explore presence of groundwater, several indicators like flora, fauna and soil texture and color were considered. The plants as indicators of groundwater are described by Suraphala. Some of these are:*Jambu or black plum, Badari, Palasha, Kasha, Munja, Bibhitaka.*

3.9 Ancient and Prehistoric Structures for Harvesting and Storing water

Construction of reservoirs for harvesting and storing water was the vital need of the arid and semi arid regions. For this a number of different structures were made and some are described below:

A. Tanka

➢ Harvesting of rain water in *Tanka* has been one of the ancient and relatively hygienic methods of water storage and has been the main source of drinking water in desert. *Tankas* were constructed on the farm, in houses, palatial buildings, etc. In forts and houses it was constructed mainly for harvesting roof water. A two meter diameter and three meter deep *Tanka* has capacity to store 10,000 liters of water.

B. Talai

- Similar to *Tanka*, *Talai* was also one of the oldest methods of harvesting rain water. *Talais* were mostly constructed in towns. A *Talai* was about 2 to 3 m deep constructed by scooping out soil. Constructed in area in which there is adequate flow of rain water into talai. The *Talai* was kept open. Pucca masonary entrance is provided. To make use of stored water, a staircase was provided in the *Talai*. In emergencies, water is poured which is brought using camel, donkey, bullock cart *etc.*

C. Nada

- *Nada* was a common reservoir for storing rain water in the villages of the Thar desert. *Nadas* were constructed on range land, barren land, or pasture land. Catchment area is 5-10 ha. Provides short term storage of rain water mainly used for animals.

D. Khadin

- *Khadin* was an ancient indigenous rain water harvesting method mainly found in arid regions. The accumulation of runoff water between hillocks is called *Khadin*. The *Khadin* water was generally used for cultivation under preserved moisture conditions and for animal consumption. Water is used for crop cultivation and animal consumption. Useful for cultivation of crops in 60-70 ha area.

E. Nadi

- Constructed on slopy area and high embankment is provided as compared to nada. Adequate cleanliness is maintained in the watershed to maintain purity of stored water. The catchment area is 10-150 ha and depth is kept upto 6-8 m. Bath is strictly prohibited. Water is available for whole of year. Therefore, nadi is a shelter home for many wild animals and birds.

F. Sar, sagar and samand

- These are refined natural water bodies. Rainwater is harvested and used for irrigation.

3.10 Invention of Irrigation

- When the primitive man learned the process of growing crops for his own necessity, the only source of getting water for his crops was rain. But, when there were no rains, he drew off water from rivers and natural lakes and in this way irrigation was invented
- In Rigveda, irrigation from wells has been mentioned. Water was raised from wells by means of a strap and water pails and also by buckets tied with a rope to one end of a long wooden pole working on the pully. The other end of the wooden pole carried a heavy weight. The water was lifted in the bucket by the gravitational force acting on the heavy weight. Such system of irrigation can be seen even today in the rural areas. The ancient people had efficient craftsman called *Ribhus* who used to dig channels from rivers to the field to carry water for irrigation
- Around 3000 BC, the farmers of Baluchistan impounded rain water by using stone rubble dams for irrigation. Similar structures have been found in Kutch, Sabarkantha and Bhavanagar in Gujarat and also near Karachi in Pakistan. Evidence of the collection of monsoon runoff is available in Cholavira, a major site of the Indus Valley Civilization
- During 4th century BC, the irrigation canals were constructed by the kings of Nanda dynasty. In the period of Chandragupta Maurya also, emphasis was given to irrigation system by constructing dams and lakes
- In 2nd century BC, Hathigumta inscriptions showed the description of the major tanks in Kalinga (modern Orissa). In Tamil Nadu, Chola king Karikalan constructed a stone dam across the river Cauvery in 100 AD. This dam is considered as master piece of engineering even today. The river water was directed to tanks for irrigation through channels.

In Ancient India the tank irrigation existed in semi arid and arid regions of India since the Vedic period. Mentions of tanks and lakes are found in Ramayana and Mahabharata. Evidence of the collection of monsoon runoff in Dholavaria, a major site of the Indus valley civilization (3000-1500 BC) is also available.

During the medieval period also around 12th Century, Ana Sagar lake was built at Ajmer. Ghadsisar reservoir lake was built at Jaisalmer in 1367 AD.

Chapter 4

Plant Protection and ITKs

"You, I, everyone on this planet is sent by God with the freedom to cultivate all creative potential within us. We differ in the way we make our choices and evolve our destiny. Life is a difficult game. You have to be willing to ignore the pressure to do things the way others say they should be done"

- Dr. A. P. J Abdul Kalam

4.1 Plant Growth and Development

Vedas represent the most sacred literature of the Vedic Indo Aryans. Of the four Vedas, Rigveda, is the oldest. In Rigveda, plant growth and development was mentioned. It was mentioned that "Sun" is the purifier and protector of everything. The "light" feed all living things. The "light" provides the whole energy. It is essential for germination of seed and plant development. The seeds germinate only in the soil. Their roots are mechanically supported by the soil. Both the aerial parts and soil parts of plants depend on *vaayu* and *varsha* for their growth and development. The ocean, the sky and the space are the three places where fire originates. Fire, in the form of Sun, has divided seasons to produce all living beings, including plants, on the earth in a sequence. The Sun who watches the whole universe provides energy required for plant life. *Grishma*, *Varsha* and *Shishir* seasons are the heart of a *samvatshar* (full year). *Vasant*, *Sharad* and *Hemanth* are the other seasons. A *samvatshar* is variable, characterized by heat, rain and cold. Full of rain produces full of grains. Samvatshar ensures growth and development of plants there by flowers and fruits. Water pleases *samvatshar* for four months and leaves it for eight months. During these four months the plants and trees grow and develop.

4.2 Some special Treatments during or after Planting

- If rose is grown near a peach tree, the fruits of the peach tree will be sweet smelling
- At the time of planting a vine cutting, if dung is applied on its lower part, it will produce roots quickly and will remain safe from insects
- If 2 or 3 eggs are bunged beneath each plant, it will produce more figs. Or if the sap of the pounded leaves of olive is sprinkled on a fig tree it will grow more figs
- Cold water should be avoided for irrigation of rice
- In pomegranate, the branches chosen for cultivation should be from the upper part of the tree and not from the surrounding parts. They should be broken by hand and not cut with a knife or blade.

4.3 Plant Protection

In ancient period the only method to protect the crops were prayers and chanting 'mantras'. This does not mean that Indians were not aware of insects and pathogens and the damage caused by them. Some of the pests affecting crops were named in Sanskrit *viz., gandhi, shankhi, pandarmundi, dhuli, shringari,* etc. It is certain that *Gandhi* (offensive odor/smell) was what is called today the Gundhi-bug (*Leptocorisa varicornis*); *shankhi* means snail; *pandarmundi* means white head which is a typical symptom of the attack of rice stem borer. Similarly *dhuli* means powder and this word was used for powdery mildew of wheat and barley. The word *shringari* indicates something adorned with red color and that the term was used for rust diseases.

Besides insects and diseases, goats, deers, rats, wild boars, pigs and sparrows were recorded as the destroyers of crops. The history of India reveals that the country has seen many ups and downs due to damages by insects. Vedas are the world's oldest literature containing knowledge on science of insects, their morphology and life cycles. This Indian literature is still present in many countries, which needs to be traced. An example of Vrikshayurveda may be quoted in this regard. This text was traced in the Bodleian Library of Oxford University, England.

A. Plant Protection in Ancient India

Plant protection began when man attempted to understand ailments affecting crops. Crop plants are affected by "abiotic" and "biotic" disorders. Insects were seen on plants more than 250 million years ago *i.e.,* well before man, who is seen since 2 million years ago.

- The association of man with insects was well known to Asians who produced silk and lac well before 3,870 B.C
- The documents available on man's efforts to protect crops by insects are found in the Rigveda
- There was mention of algae and mushrooms in Rigveda as Saprophytes
- Susruta emphasized the importance of protecting seeds from white ants
- Kautilya was the first to suggest use of seed dressers for producing healthy plant stand
- In Kallavagga, a Buddhist document, there was mention of "mildew of paddy" and "blight of sugarcane"
- In *Krishi Parashara*, crop losses due to pests were mentioned and for plant protection prayers were offered to God Indra and other supernaturals
- In Verse 126 of *Krishi Parashara*, it was mentioned that commencing ploughing on the 14th day of the month in any agricultural season is auspicious and reduced several losses by insect pests
- Auspicious "lagnas" for initiating agricultural activities in a particular season such as Taurus (21st April) were fixed based on the moment of the Sun's entrance into the respective Zodiac sign
- In Kautilya's Artha Shastra it was mentioned that organic materials were used to control crop disorders. Example: cut ends of sugarcane setts meant for planting were plastered with a mixture of honey, ghee, the fat of hogs and cow dung
- Varahamihira suggested the use of milk, ghee and cow dung for dressing seeds and smoking them by burning animal flesh or turmeric before sowing

- Placing a mixture of flowers of cereals, legumes and sesame as well as meat was practiced to control pests
- Botanical pesticides, neem leaves were commonly used to control storage insects and seed infection during storage
- There was also mention about the use of seed treatment with coal ash before storage to prevent insect damage during storage
- Sun drying of Pigeonpea seeds before storage was a common practice during ancient period for the management of insect pests

B. Plant Protection in Vrikshayurveda

In Vrikshayurveda, Surapala has given plant protection techniques in a very systematic manner right from seed treatment to the storage of grains. Therefore, this period is considered as the starting point of systematic plant protection in Indian agricultural heritage.

- *Ailments described by Surapala*
    - Diseases of all kinds of trees are two types *viz.,* internal and external. It is unfortunate that all textbooks on plant pathology give credit to the French botanist Tournefort (1705 AD), for classifying diseases–internal and external. This was more than 700 years after Surapala had already done such a classification. The internal ones are caused by the imbalance of *vata*, *pitta*, and *kafa;* and external ones are caused by insects, cold weather, *etc*.
    - The diseases caused by *vata* are due to the land that becomes arid on account of excessive supply of dry and pungent matter. This leads to thinness and crookedness of trunk, appearance of knots on trunks of trees, and the fruits become hard with less juice and less sweetness
    - The diseases of *pitta* occur at the end of summer if trees are excessively watered with materials which are bitter, sour, salty and strong. These are characterized by yellowness of leaves, dropping of fruits, dryness, paleness of flowers and fruit, and decay
    - The diseases of *kafa* type occur in winter and spring if the trees are excessively watered with materials which are sweet, oily, sour or cold. Affected trees take long time to bear fruits, dwarfing of leaves, tastelessness and pre maturity

- It is interesting to note that no attempt was made in the world by which plant disorders were classified into two groups- internal and external, before the time of Surapala. Further, it is very significant that physiology of trees was considered similar to those of humans and therefore, the internal disorders were classified into *vata, pitta* and *kafa* types as had been done in case of humans that are the *tridosha* principle. Many symptoms described by Surapala can be attributed today to diseases caused by fungi, bacteria or nematodes. In addition, damage due to other non infectious causes (external) such as excessive heat, frost, mechanical injuries, drought or water logging, birds, excessive growth of creepers and competition by weeds was recognized.

4.4 Ancient Plant Protection Practices Still Followed in India

In traditional agricultural practices, farmers evolved an effective system of crop protection through generations of experience and intimate knowledge of their environment. Some of these indigenous practices are still followed by the farmers in different parts of the country.

A. Plant protection in Arunachal Pradesh

Several indigenous practices of plant protection such as rituals, use of plant extracts, storage management, *etc.*, are still followed in Arunachal Pradesh. Some of these are:

- *Buttermilk for pest control*: Farmers treat garlic seeds with buttermilk @ 10-12 litres ha^{-1} before sowing for protection against different diseases and insect pests
- *Asafoetida to control ergot of sorghum*: Asafoetida (50-60 g) is mixed in water and the solution is used to treat sorghum seeds for protection against ergot
- *Control of ginger rot and yellowing*: The tribal farmers sow ginger after treating with a solution of cow dung. About 10-15 kg cow dung and asafoetida (40-80 g) are mixed in 8-10 liters of water. This is enough to treat ginger rhizomes required for one hectare. This practice is helpful for protecting ginger plants from rotting during vegetative growth. To prevent yellowing, the farmers grow papaya as an intercrop for providing shade to ginger. The leaves of ginger do not turn yellow and high yields are obtained

- *Control of tomato wilt*: Farmers use turmeric powder @ 15-20 grams per litre of water to control wilt (*Fusarium* sp.) of tomato. This solution is used to treat the roots of seedlings in tomato nursery before transplanting
- *Control of early stem borer in sugarcane*: To control stem borer (*Chilo infuscatellus*) in sugarcane, farmers use neem oil @ 1.5-2 litres ha^{-1}. This practice is repeated thrice in the whole period of sugarcane vegetative growth
- *Control of termites*: Farmers keep asafoctida in a pack of cotton cloth at two or three points in the irrigation channel of 10-15 meters for controlling termites (*Odonotermes* spp.) in affected crops
- *Control of storage pests*: Farmers use different simple practices for effective control of storage pests *viz.,* fuel wood ash at 250 g for 250 kg of pluses; dry neem leaves @ 2.5 kg for 100 kg of wheat; and 5 to 6 dry chillies placed in one kg seed of mung bean and blackgram.

B. Plant protection in semi-arid region of Rajasthan

The following methods of plant protection are used by farming communities in the semi-arid region of Rajasthan, since ancient times:

- Control of termites
    - Termite attack and cracking of epidermis in fruits can be avoided by using a paste on the main trunk with a mixture of mustard oil (one liter) and turmeric powder (200 g). Mustard oil attracts ants which remove termites while turmeric powder helps in healing the cracks. In another practice, *aak* (*Calotropis* sp.) leaves are chopped, filled in gunny bags, and kept in irrigation channel. The exudates from these leaves kill termites and other soil borne pathogens
    - Famers amend the soil with the pre incubated mixture of *aak* leaves (5 bags), neem kernels and leaves (95 bags), and asafoetida (200 g) to check termite attack in the field and soil borne diseases. Farmers are benefited through good growth of crops due to this amendment
- Control of *Helicoverpa*
    - To control *Helicoverpa* in chickpea, farmers followed a typical bio-control method. Pearlmillet grains or pieces of *chapatti* (thin unleavened bread) soaked in buttermilk are scattered in chickpea field to attract birds, which in turn predate on *Helicoverpa* larvae.

Further, neem leaves and kernels are being commonly used to control the pest (*Helicoverpa*) on cotton and chickpea in some areas.

- Spraying of extract obtained by crushing together garlic, onion and chilli after dilution also effectively controls *Helicoverpa* on vegetables.

➢ Control of Thrips, Aphids, Whitefly and Other pests

To prevent thrips and aphids, cow dung ash is applied on foliage of vegetables, *e.g.,*chilli, onion, garlic and cucurbits.To trap insects like whitefly and thrips, spraying of buttermilk over cucurbits and chilli plant is a common practice in some districts of Rajasthan

➢ In Jodhpur district some farmers use cow urine based biopesticide to check whitefly, jassids, and other sucking pests of chilli and cumin (*jeera*). This is prepared by mixing cow urine (10 L), neem kernel and leaves (2 kg), and garlic (50 g). The ingredients are crushed and kept in a copper container for 15 days. The solution is then heated till 5 litres of solution is left. After cooling, the liquid is filtered and diluted with 500 litres of water before sowing. The farmers even claimed its efficacy in controlling viral diseases of chilli.

➢ Control of Nematodes

A mixture of cow dung, leaves of *aak* (*Calotropis* sp.), foliage of *kheip*or *khip* (*Crotalaria burhai* a local xerophytic plant) is allowed to rot in a pit for about two months. This mixture (manure) is then applied in chilli and tomato fields for control of root-knot nematodes and termites and for good plant growth.

C. Plant protection by tribal farmers in Rajasthan

The following methods of plant protection are used by tribal farmers in Rajasthan.

➢ In paddy, a solution of 4 litres of cow urine and 10 g asafoetida in 10 litres of water is sprayed to repel sucking pests (aphids and jassids)

➢ To control paddy blast and bacterial blight, farmers spray a solution of cow dung prepared by mixing 3 kg cow dung in 3 litres of water

➢ In case of insect holes made by shoot borer and bark eaters in mango trees, jaggery is placed in the holes to attract other predators (ants), which will feed on the insects present in the holes. Farmers also pour kerosene in the insect holes or block the holes with cow dung

- A particular method of controlling fungal diseases on chillies is practiced by tribals in which the twigs of *aak* (*Calotropis* sp.) are placed in between rows. Some other farmers place fresh cow dung near the collar region of chilli plant to prevent it from fungal diseases *viz.,* damping off and die back
- In case of soil borne diseases such as root rot and collar rot, and termite attack, castor, *karanja* (*Pongamia pinnata*), neem cakes are used as control measures
- During sprouting of sugarcane setts the stem of *aak* (*Calotropis* spp.) is placed in the irrigation channel during intercultural operations. This is effective against termites.

D. Plant Protection in Tea estates in Northeast India

Recently, based on Surapala's Vrikshayurveda, Valmiki Sreenivasa Iyengar used different preparations, *viz., Panchagavya, Chimmigavya, Dhanyagavya, Indsafari, etc.,* having effective insecticidal and fungicidal properties against tea bushes in Northeast India.

- *Control of Tea mosquito bug (Helopeltis theivora)*

The method followed at in Tea Estates of Assam.

- Fresh leaves of *Vitex negundo* and *Clerodendrum serratum* are chopped into small pieces and filled up to the brim in a 200 litre barrel. Then raw cow dung (20 kg) and molasses (2 kg) are added to it and the barrel is filled with water upto the top and stirred well. The barrel is closed with the lid and allowed to ferment for 12-15 days. It is filtered and used in desired concentrations, as decoction
- This decoction is found very effective against *Helopeltis* at all concentrations. Spraying at weekly intervals at 2% concentration controlled this dreaded pest in tea plantation.

4.5 Introduction to ITKs

The term "Indigenous Technical Knowledge (ITK)" is used as synonym to 'local' and 'traditional' knowledge to differentiate it from 'scientific', 'modern' and 'rational' knowledge. The ITK products on agriculture in India are strong knowledge pools developed by different communities through keen observations, natural selection and centuries of trial and error. Those ITKs that were proved effective and sustainable on a long term basis to counter the stresses and helped reap better harvest existed through hundreds of years of adaptive evolution in India. Even though in many cases the ITKs on agriculture are 'unwritten' they did exist in different brains, languages and skills with innumerable communities and cultures because the ITKs helped for successful and persistent adoption to the environment. In modern India, this knowledge on agriculture is not utilized to its capacity in reducing the dependence on costlier external inputs and in evolving coping strategies to propogate an eco-friendly agriculture so far. Therefore, there is a need to blend ITK on agriculture with modern agriculture and this is termed as "Blended Technology (BT)", which helps in successfully facing the tremendous odds of often harsh and inimical stresses and climatic conditions and to plan crops and cropping patterns in advance while minimizing the risk due to vagaries of monsoon rains and climate change in India. Also, these BTs provide a powerful basis from which alternate ways of managing agricultural resources can be developed.

A. Practices using ITKs

- Mulching with Neem leaves/paddy straw @ 6 q ha^{-1} for soft rot disease in Ginger
- Karanja oil cake @ 100-150 q ha^{-1} for fungal and bacterial infection in Ginger
- Red mud + wood ash (equal proportion) for scale insect and better keeping quality in Ginger
- For Control of *cascuta* in Niger
    - Jackfruit leaf abstract @ 1.25 litres of water applied 40 DAS
    - Seed treatment with kerosene @ 3 ml kg^{-1} of seed and kept overnight
    - Mixed showing of Ragi + Niger (1:10 ratio)

4.6 Examples of Traditional Knowledge in Crop Production using ITKs

- Rainfed rice cultivation in the eastern state of West Bengal, India is highly complex, risky and uncertain due to insufficient or excess early or late rains, early or late floods and their erratic withdrawal, etc. Therefore, the farmers adopt certain traditional methods to minimize the losses of crops due to these weather abnormalities. They sow a mixture of both autumn and winter rice varieties to ensure that a good harvest of at least one variety in the event of these weather aberrations. Also, they use staggered nursery for transplanting in the main field because the cost of nursery raising is less and under flooded conditions they also transplant lengthy and aged seedlings to overcome the submergence. Similarly, to meet the optimum date of sowing, they sow the seed as soon as the summer rains are received and take the advantage of initial soil moisture for germination

- In dryland areas of northern India the delayed, erratic distribution and untimely rains are the serious problems for cultivation of wheat in winter (November) and maize in rainy season (June). In winter, if excessive early rains are received it will not be possible to sow wheat crop because, due to low air and soil temperatures the drying of excessive soil moisture takes atleast one month. Therefore, traditionally farmers follow "dry sowing" method in which the seeds are sown in the soil by taking the advantage of initial soil moisture of late SW monsoon rains. The seeds remain healthy in the soil and germinate when enough rains are received. Similar method of early sowing in May is followed for maize crop also which helps the farmers to overcome the difficulty of sowing number of times and meeting the optimum date of sowing in the event of untimely rains
- Cultivation of cucurbits, melons, gourds, etc., in sandy soils of southern, northern and north western India is risky and uncertain. In northern India the seedlings of these vegetables are grown in poly bags and allowed to grow in trenches to protect them from frost damage. The same seedling are transplanted in the main field during February second fortnight and farmers reap bumper harvest. However, in contrast in southern India the fully grown fruits of these vegetables are put in trenches along with their tendrils and twigs to prevent their cracking and damage due to high air and soil temperatures

- The Indian dryland farmers also developed another Indigenous Technical Weather Knowledge to overcome the menace of heavy infestation by pests and diseases on vegetables grown in off-season. In northern India the farmers raise nurseries of vegetables in November (early winter) and take the advantage of enough soil temperature for germination. However, the growth of these seedlings is restricted till January due to low soil and air temperatures in winter. The transplanting of seedlings is taken up in February such that the main field crops grow under optimum weather conditions and yield potentially. If the seedlings are grown in February (late winter) the flowering and fruiting synchronizes with the onset of monsoon rains and the pests and disease menace cause heavy or total loss of crops.

The above methods were being followed in India sincc timcs immemorial.

4.7 Examples of Traditional Knowledge in Water management using ITKs

The entire Indian landscape is dotted with hundreds and thousands of lakes and ponds. The following are the few examples of traditional knowledge in water management

- The traditional system of rain water harvesting for irrigation still prevails in several parts of India, especially in remote villages. Farm field bundings by "Earthern bunds" is a popular method of rain water harvesting in India. In this system a series of earthen bunds are constructed across the farm land according to slope of the land to stop runoff water. Bunds help in storing water and also assist in controlling soil and water erosion
- Hand irrigation from numerous water tanks, wells and ditches is a practice in India which still continues in rural areas. In this system water is drawn manually with simple device called" Piccotah". The system works very smoothly with minimum strain and can irrigate 4-5 ha of land every day
- "Surangam" is a fresh water harvesting structure in vogue in the western ghats of northern Malabar. These are basically tunnels dug through lateritic soil hillocks from the periphery of which water or

moisture seeps out. One does not require any energy to get water from them and most often the water is of good quality. Initial expenditure for digging "surangam" is the only expenditure and it hardly requires any maintenance. These are carried from generation to generation. These are used for agriculture in dry areas

- Tanks and ponds formed an integral part of the traditional irrigation system in Kerala.

Chapter 5

Medicinal Plants and Seed Health

"The best way to win is to not feel that desperate need to win. The best performances are accomplished when you are relaxed and free of doubt"

- Dr. A. P. J Abdul Kalam

5.1 Heritage of Medicinal Plants and their Relevance Today

Ayurveda, the "Indian science of life" was theorized before a few thousand years and was practiced since then upto this day. Although in theory the science relates to all forms of life, in actual practice, its efficacy is widely known only in the case of human beings.

Ayurveda, which is also the sacred knowledge of life, originated when diseases cropped up and posed impediments to penance, abstinence, study, religious observances and life span of living beings. Holy sages, with superior intellect sharpened by spiritual powers, acquired the eternal knowledge from divine tradition and, out of mercy for all living things on earth, brought it to the terrestrial level.

A. Basic Principles and Concepts of Ayurveda

- Plants and trees along with the rest of the physical world, are evolved from the five elements viz., thunder (sky) soil, wind, fire and water
- The three humors – vata (wind), pitta (bile), and kapha (phlegm) – are also evolved from the five elements but are manifest only in the four life forms. (humans and animals, serpents and birds, insects and pests, and plants and trees). They form the basis of Ayurveda

- All living organisms are a replica of the vast external universe, and are as such constituted of the five elements of the universe,– sky, soil, wind, fire and water. There are two forces in the universe – the hot and the cold, which are constantly changing it. The third force vayu (wind) which activates these two forces and balances and regulates their functioning
- Despite the fact that all the five elements are present in the constitution of all the three humors (doshas), wind is dominant in vata, fire in pitta, and water in the constitution of kapha. The tridoshas have their characteristic attributes due to the dominant elements. Thus, vata is dry, light, cool, rough, subtle and motion-prone by nature. Pitta is slightly sharp, hot, light, foul-smelling, flowing, and liquid in nature. Kapha is cool, heavy, sluggish, smooth, sticky and immobile by nature. The equilibrium of these three in a living organism translates into health, which is the main purpose of ayurveda
- The ayurveda shastra has identified certain common causative factors responsible for health and disease
- The golden precept of ayurveda is "prevention is better than cure"
- The treatment mainly consists of administering substances with attributes opposite to the respective vitiated dosha
- Diseases occur either by aggravation or attenuation of dosha
- Treatment materials are selected in ayurveda because they 'act' as remedies for the respective diseases. Materials 'act' through five conduit. These are
    - Rasa (taste)
    - Guna (quality)
    - Virya (potency)
    - Vipaka (culmination)
    - Prabhava (efficacy)
- For the purpose of administration, the treatment materials are used in five different forms – juice, paste, decoction and cold and hot infusion
- In administering materials to treat diseases, one of the concepts of ayurveda is that along with life, plants also have a definite body structure like humans

- It is worth noting that the *Mantra* against pests is only intended to drive them out and not to destroy them. Taking resort to prayer is indicative of admission of the limited power of human efforts against pests
- When a patient does not respond to any treatment, he is advised a change of place and climate. In the same manner, a tree that does not respond to any treatment is transplanted
- The universally accepted principle that 'love and tender care are as important as medical treatment,' is clearly reflected even in the case of trees, in the text of Vrikshayurveda.

Besides these basic principles, Surapala has extended many other theories and concepts of ayurveda to plants while prescribing remedies for their ailments.

5.2 Pomegranate- A High Value Medicinal Fruit Tree

The pomegranate, *Punica granatum* L. Puniaceae), is the traditional fruit of the central Iranian plateau, where it originated. Historical evidence suggests that man first began planting pomegranate trees sometime between 4000 and 3000 BC. There is no other fruit crop that has a medicinal value as high as that of the pomegranate. The pomegranate grows from Iran to the Himalayas in northern India and has been cultivated and naturalized over the whole Mediterranean region since ancient times. From the nuclear area of the Fertile crescent the pomegranate spread eastwards into India and China, and westwards into Spain. This fruit of myth has been used in many cultures, particularly in the Middle east and India, to treat inflammation, rheumatism and sore throats, and also to slow the ageing process.

A. Uses of pomegranate

- Antioxidant and food uses
  - Pomegranate is known for its antioxidants, which eliminate harmful free radicals in the body. The antioxidants in pomegranate prevent oxidation and hence increase longevity
  - In India, the pomegranate has long been regarded as a food medicine of great importance. All parts of the tree, the roots, the reddish brown bark, leaves, flowers, rind, and kernels have featured in medicine for thousands of years

- The medical authorities of ancient India described it as a light food and a tonic for the heart
- The ancient medical writers of Arabia considered sweet pomegranate varieties a good laxative and varieties intermediate between sweet and sour as good for inflammation of the stomach and pain for the heart.

➢ Digestive disorders

Pomegranate juice is of great value in digestive disorders. It is an appetizer, a digestive food item, and is useful for patients suffering from colitis and mucus.

➢ Diarrhoea and dysentery

The chief value of the pomegranate is its astringent property which causes cells to shrink, and it is a valuable food medicine for diarrhoea and dysentery in both humans and animals.

➢ Sore eyes

The crushed pomegranate flowers when made paste relieve sore eyes. This remedy was particularly resorted to in Ceylon (now Srilanka).

➢ Intestinal worms

The bark, both of the root and the stems of the pomegranate tree, destroy parasitic worms.

➢ Fevers

The juice of the fruit with the addition of a little saffron is useful in fevers to allay thirst.

➢ Itching

The skin of the pomegranate fruit is considered highly beneficial in the treatment of itching.

➢ Kidney and bladder stones

The kernels of sour and sweet pomegranate are useful as a medicine. A tablespoon of kernels, ground into a fine paste can be given along with a cupful of horsegram soup to dissolve gravel in kidney and bladder.

- Tooth and gum disorders

  Powder of the dry rind mixed with pepper and common salt is applied as a very good dentifrice, i.e., toothpaste or powder. Its regular application strengthens the gums, stops bleeding, prevents pyorrhea, cleans the teeth and preserves them for a long time.

B. Some folk Remedies with Pomegranate

Some folk remedies from villages in southern Gujarat on pomegranate are:

- Boil 100 g of pomegranate rind in 4 cups of water. Use this infusion to brush teeth every morning to treat gum inflammation and purulent infections
- Boil the rind of the fruit and rinse mouth with this infusion 2 to 3 times a day to disinfect tonsils and throat and treat canker sores
- Soak 50g of dry pomegranate root bark overnight in 1 or 2 glasses of cold water. Boil it for a few minutes the following morning, let it cool and drink 2 or 3 times at 15 minute intervals to expel *Taenia solium*, the tapeworm.

5.3 Seed Health in Ancient and Medieval History and its Relevance to Present day Agriculture

A. Verses according to Parashara on seed health

The term "seed health" refers primarily to the presence or absence of disease-causing organisms such as fungi, bacteria, viruses, nematodes and insects. However, physiological conditions such as trace element deficiency may be involved.

- Proper season (*ritu*), good soil (*kshetra*), water (*ambu*), and vigorous seed (*vija*), together with proper care, help the emergence of strong and non-diseased sprouts
- All sorts of seeds should be procured in *Magha* (February) or *Phalguna* (March) and should then be dried well in the sun without putting those directly on the ground
- While putting the seeds in a small pouch, seeds of other plants as well as straw must be removed from it. A mixture of different kinds of seeds cause great loss

- Uniform seeds produce excellent results. Hence, every effort should be made to procure uniform seeds
- While putting the seeds in a strong bag, the farmer should weed out grass that shoots out (in the field). If grass is not weeded it spreads later, growing all over the farm
- Seeds should never be stored in a place beset with white ants or in a cowshed
- The farmer should not even by mistake place ghee, oil, buttermilk, lamp, or salt on the seeds
- Seeds which have come in contact with lamp, fire, or smoke and which are exposed to rain or stored in a pit should always be discarded
- Seeds which are pressed or are mixed with other inferior matter should never, even by mistake, be sown. Seeds blended with inferior matter or with leftover food grains do not sprout even if sown
- Seeds which become non-viable turn everything including the farmer, the manure, the furrow, the oxen, and the multitude of rain-clouds into barrenness
- The "origin of plentiful yield" is the seed
- These directions are useful in sowing the seeds of sesame, rice, and barley. One should therefore, put in maximum effort to procure and preserve these seeds.

B. Verses According to Kautilya on seed health

- The seeds are to be exposed to night-mist and day-heat for seven consecutive days. The practice of exposing seed to dew in the night and drying it under sun during the day is certainly interesting. Before systemic fungicides became available to farmers in 1960s to control internally seedborne smut diseases in cereals, soaking seed in water to activate fungal mycelia and drying the seed under hot sun to kill these activated mycelia was a recommended practice for wheat seed in northern India to control the loose smut disease. It is possible that the practice mentioned by Kautilya could be leading to activation of fungi and bacteria present on seed surface or just under the seed coat and then followed by their death on exposure to sun, and thus the seed was freed from potential pathogens

- Cut ends of sugarcane setts were plastered with a mixture of honey, ghee, hog fat, and cowdung. Honey is mildly antimicrobial; ghee and hog fat could "seal off" cut ends from contaminated soil as well as prevent loss of moisture from the setts, and cowdung could promote biocontrol of potential pathogens.

C. A verse according to Varahamihira

- All seeds (of trees, shrubs, creepers) should be soaked in milk for 10 days, taking them out with the hand smeared with ghee. Then they must be rolled many times in cowdung, fumigated with the flesh of deer and hog; thereafter with flesh and hog's marrow, they should be planted in a soil that has been already prepared. Being sprinkled with milk and water the seeds will grow and bloom.

D. Seed health in Hellenistic age (Greek/Roman civilizations)

The Hellenistic age extends from the time after the death of Alexander the Great (323 BC) to about 500AD. The verses on seed health in this age are as follows:

- According to Theophrastus (372-285BC) some seeds such as millet germinate quickly and keep well. Beans rot soon. Barley perishes sooner than wheat seed. Dusty grains deteriorate faster than clean grain
- According to Varro (116-27BC) beans and other legumes keep well for long time when they are covered with a layer of ashes and are kept in an olive jar.

E. Seed health in India

- In the Indian civilization Susruta emphasized “strong and non-diseased sprouts”
- As mentioned above, Parashara recommended proper drying of seed, free from weeds etc.,
- Again as mentioned above, Kautilya was the first to suggest seed treatment with cowdung, honey and ghee to ensure good germination and emergence.

F. Materials Recommended for Seed Treatments

Many substances were recommended for seed treatment at various times by scholars of different civilizations

- Ash and animal excreta like cowdung and fumigation with burning of animal flesh was used by the Indians
- Silkworm droppings and sheep dung was used by Chinese. They also used horse bone soup for seed pelleting
- Animal urine was suggested by Romans for seed treatment.

5.4 Traditional Experiments on Seed Germination

Seeds, both green and dry are considered living bodies. They do get hurt or even die when subjected to ill treatment such as trauma, high temperature, fall from a great height etc. Seeds also die or become infertile because of boiling or baking. It is only the live seeds that germinate and dead ones do not.

Experimental indications of seed germination and crop growth in India

- In a traditional practice a pot with seeds sown are laid in front of the Godess during "Chaitragouri" and "Navaratri". On the last day of the festival in each home, a few seedlings are picked up, washed to remove soil from the roots and the proportion of growth of shoot and root is observed. Afterwards every sown pot is taken out in a procession round the village by the respected mother of the house on her head. The keen eyes of sons, daughters who have seen the extent of growth at their homes would know the extent of growth in each direction of the village, as they know the residential home and place of each respected mother of the house who is carrying piously the pot. The children and respected and honoured villagers can foretell crop growth pattern in each direction of the village. "Chaitragouri" pots indicate Kharif growth and while "Navratri" pots indicate rabi growth
- *Mandvan*: Another experimental method of forecasting crop growth is called *mandvan.* The decision is taken in the Ashadha month's Krishna paksha, when the Moon is just out of *rohini nakshtra*. Seeds of all the crops to be sown are collected from every house in the village in measured quantity. Three days

in advance of the Moon's entering *Rohini* of *Ashadha Krishna Paksha*, these seeds are sown in four red earthen pots. The pots are placed in a mandav, or tent, in the east, west, north and south of the tent. After 4 to 5 days, the seeds are removed and from the germination percentage, predictions are made about the performance of each crop during that year. A high germination percentage is the indicator of good crop growth.

Chapter 6

Civilization- Journey in Agriculture

"There are boundaries that dictate life. One shall accept destiny and go ahead with life. However, with faith one can change his destiny"

- Dr. A. P. J Abdul Kalam

6.1 Indian Civilization

Ancient life was agriculture based. Ancient festivals were agriculture based. Ancient food habits and way of life were agriculture based. Agriculture was not only an important occupation of the farmers, but also their way of life, culture and custom.

A. Sindhu – Saraswathi Civilization

India is separated from other countries by the world's highest mountains, the Himalayas. In ancient times the only route from India to other lands was through these mountain passes in the Northwest. Nearly the whole Indian Peninsula is a table land. Between table land and Himalayas lie the plains. The "Sindhu river" flows through the western part of the plain and the "Ganges river" through the eastern part. Both the rivers have their origin in the Himalayas. They flood large areas when snow melts in the mountains.

➢ *Phases of Sindhu- Saraswati Civilisation*

The four phases of Sindhu- Saraswati civilization are

- Saraswati (8000- 3300 BC)
- Early Harappan (3300-2800 BC)
- Mature Harappan (2800-1900 BC)
- Late Harappan (1900-1400BC)

Harappan civilization is also known as "Indus civilization". In this civilization, farmers utilised pots and utensils. Farmers identified the importance of ploughing for proper sowing of crops. They also found that soil has to be covered over the seeds sown. Ox drawn wheel cart was used for transport of agricultural produce. Farmers cultivated several crops and devised methods of cotton ginning, spinning and weaving. Animals were domesticated and used in agriculture. The most remarkable discovery in Indus civilization is, great granaries used for storing food grains.

B. ***Vedic civilization***

➢ *Origin of Aryans*

The name "Aryan" is derived from the Indo-European root word "ar" meaning "noble". The Aryans called themselves "noble ones" or "superior ones" to distinguish themselves from the people they conquered. The Aryans entered India from central Asia in the 2nd millennium BC. The Aryan land was called "saptasindhava", which means the land of seven rivers. These rivers were 1. Sutudri (Sutlej); 2.Vipas (Beas); 3.Parushni (Ravi); 4.Asikni (Chenab); 5.Vitasta (Jhelum) 6. Sindhu (Indus) and 7.Saraswati (which disappeared long ago).

Aryans were more prevalent during the Vedic time which covers eastern Afghanistan, Kashmir, Punjab, parts of Sindh and Rajasthan. Rigveda was the oldest book of Aryans.

➢ *Vedas*

Vedas are the oldest literature in the world. The word Veda is derived from "vid" which means "knowledge". Vedas are only literary source that indicates the presence of Aryans in India. Vedas include four compilations

- Rigveda (includes hymns)
- Yajurveda (includes hymns and rituals)
- Samaveda (includes re-composition of Rigveda for singing)
- Atharvanaveda (includes charm *i.e.,* magic power against spirits and diseases)

Vedas are full of scientific knowledge and compilation of studies made by sages for innumerable years after collecting data. The

Vedic literature recalls a high level of civilization which was present much earlier than Greek and other civilizations of the world. The famous French philosopher Voltaire said "vedas are the most precious gift for which the Western countries have ever been indebted to the Eastern countries".

When Swami Vivekananda visited USA in 1901, he spoke on vedas and vedanta and acquainted Americans with physical, chemical and other active properties of material substances in vedas.

➢ *Vedic periods*

- Pre- Vedic period : before 3100 BC
- 1st phase of Vedic Period: 3100 BC
- 2nd phase of Vedic Period: 2150 BC
- 3rd phase of Vedic Period: 2150 BC to 1400 BC
- 4th Vedic Jyotish Period: 1400 BC to 1200 BC

➢ *Aryans and agriculture*

During the vedic period the main occupation of the people was agriculture and the cultivated land was called "urvara". Bullocks were used to plough the land. The land belonged to community. There were channels for irrigation. People had knowledge of the practices of crop production. They were aware of seed, sowing, harvesting and threshing as was evident from the following verses:

- "to plough with bullocks join the yokes; sow the seed; let the food produced be sufficient and let the sickle be used for harvesting"
- "til (sesame) dhan (rice) masoor (lentil) and urd (black gram) were grown in abundance and these were also used during religious ceremonies".

Vedic Aryans were primarily pastoral. They cut the jungles and build their villages. They grazed the animals in jungles and cultivated barley nearest to houses to protect from wild animals. Vedic people realised the importance of off season ploughing and they started ploughing when first rains of the season were received. The first ploughing of the season was inaugurated amidst much ritual. Use of wells for drinking water, channels for irrigation was existing. Sickles were used for harvesting and sieves were used for cleaning.

Aryans possessed the knowledge of fertility of land, selection of seed, seed treatment, harvesting, manuring and rotation of crops. Aryans were accustomed to barley diet and used cotton and wool clothes.

6.2 Agriculture and Art

- The ancient Indians did all agricultural activities as art. The farmers reclaimed the lands for crops in the Ganges valley step by step. They dug the canals and ploughed the land. With abundant moisture and warmth, the fertile soil yielded good harvests for the farmers
- The iron plough share and spades were used to till the hard soils as well. Oxen were used in ploughing. Agriculture began to spread to India's table land too
- The Indians grew rice, cotton, sugarcane etc. Cotton was used to make fine fabric. The dress made out of the strong and fine fabric was so thin that a whole dress could easily pass through a small ring
- The Indians had cattle and horses. The wild chicken was domesticated in India. The elephants were used to uproot the trees, carry people and loads
- Writings emerged in India between 3000 and 2000 BC. The people used to write on datepalm leaves, cutting them into rectangles. The writings were forgotten due to the destruction of ancient cities
- Indian cities began to grow rapidly from the middle of 1st millennium BC. The largest city was Pataliputra (now Patna) on the bank of Ganga river.

6.3 Prehistoric Cropping Pattern

A. Introduction

- Water is an essential commodity for life and agriculture. Hence, the ancient civilizations of the world developed and thrived on the banks of rivers such as Indian civilization on the banks of Saraswati and Sindhu, Egyptian civilization on the banks of Nile, Chinese civilization on the banks of Huanghe and Yangtze, and Mesopotamian civilization on the banks of Euphrates and Tigris rivers. The ancestors very well recognised the importance of water to crops for irrigation. In Rigveda, earth and sky are referred to as the "mother" and "father" providing food and water to all living beings.

B. Role of Pre-Historic Cropping pattern

- In pre-historic India the southwest Asian cereals and legumes were sown as winter season crops, whereas indigenous and African crops sown in rainy season
- African millets are more productive than indigenous millets. Some sites did not grow crops in winter, while others had only winter cultivation
- Exotic crops did not all diffuse together, but moved in sequence so that naked barley arrived after hulled barley, bread wheat after dwarf and club wheats, several legume species one after another, fingermillet after sorghum, and pearlmillet after fingermillet
- Indigenous crops were also cultivated not all at one stage, but there was a sequential cultivation, viz., cereals and legumes before oilseed crops and vegetables
- Crops suited to drylands and wetlands were recognized for cultivation in both seasons, leading to the best land use. There were also choices between cereals (barley being more drought resistant than wheat) oilseeds (sesame, rape, mustard, and safflower serving different culinary purposes), millets and legumes as food
- Legumes (exotic and indigenous) were grown under rainfed conditions, but they differ in drought resistance
- Farmers could decide their cropping pattern based on their culinary (cooking) preferences and land use
- Looking at both the origins and long term histories of agricultural systems in pre-historic India, it is obvious that the indigenous crops played an important role
- Indian farmers had a very analytic mind to use appropriate cropping patterns for sustainable agricultural production.

6.4 Agriculture According to Kautilya's Artha Shastra

Being the basic component of human society, agriculture has been given high importance by Kautilya. He grouped all the industries into two categories according to their ownership; first, owned by the "state" and second owned "privately". Agriculture was placed in the category of privately owned industry. Although agriculture was placed in the private sector, Kautilya clearly mentioned that the production, distribution and consumption of agricultural products would be controlled by the king.

A. Agriculture

Kautilya gave great emphasis to agriculture and suggested a separate post of Head of Agriculture (Superintendent) and named it "*Sitadhyaksha*" who was made accountable to the state for all the farming practices.

- Land use
    - The Aartha Shastra of Kautilya gave much importance to land reform and land use which were very crucial in agricultural development. The whole cultivable land must be cultivated and no piece of cultivable land should remain unsown
    - The fields left uncultivated by the king or private owner because of shortage of manpower should be given for cultivation to those who are ready to cultivate the land for half the share in the produce (*Ardhasitika*)
    - The land may also be given to those who share any physical work for one-fifth share of the produce obtained. Kautilya knew that land left unsown would ultimately affect the production adversely.
- Rainfall
    - Although there were irrigated lands, yet a major area was rainfed. Kautilya described that 16 *dronas* (1*drona* = 6.4 cm) rainfall is sufficient for high yields of crops in dry areas whereas in humid areas 24 *dronas* rainfall would be optimum for high water required crop like rice
    - For regional crops, he mentioned that 13.5 *dronas* for Ashmaka (Marathwada region of Maharashtra), 23 *dronas* for Avanti (Malwa plateau in West Madhya Pradesh) would be optimum. The Aparanta (Konkan region of Maharashtra) and Himalayan regions get immense quantity of rain
    - Depending upon rainfall in different regions the crops were sown by *Sitadhyaksha*. Kautilya has described the technique for measuring rainfall in detail. For this a circular vessel with a diameter equal to the length of a human arm and a depth equal to the distance measured by the width of eight fingers was used to collect water

- When this vessel was filled with rain water, collected in open space, rainfall was measured to be 50 *palas* or 1 *adhaka* or ¼ *drone* (1*adhaka*= 1.6 cm in modern units)
- Although Parashara described the technique for measurement of rainfall by identifying the type of "ruling clouds", it was somewhat primitive and difficult to understand. The method of measuring rainfall by Kautilya represents a higher stage of evolution and due to its simple and refined form, it was acceptable to the agricultural community.

➢ Seed

- Kautilya considered seed as the most important component of agriculture and therefore, gave much emphasis on the procurement of quality seeds, their preservation, production and distribution
- The *Sitadhyaksha* was made accountable to collect the good quality seeds and preserve them properly so that these may be made available for agriculturists at the time of sowing.

➢ Cropping pattern

- The *Sitadhyaksha* shall grow wet crops (*kedara*), winter crops (*haimana*) and summer crops (*graishmik*) depending on the supply of water and manpower. These three crop seasons are now called *kharif* (rainy season), *rabi* (post rainy season) and *ziad* (summer), respectively. The terms *kharif, rabi* and *ziad* are Arabic words
- Kautilya categorized rice as the best crop for cultivation. Vegetable crops were considered intermediate and sugarcane as last choice because it is difficult to grow and is subjected to various evils (pests and diseases)
- Regarding other crops he mentioned that banks of rivers are suitable for growing cucurbits (*valliphala*). Lands that are frequently over flown by water are suitable for the cultivation of long pepper, grapes and sugarcane. Vegetable and root crops should be cultivated near wells. Lowlands for green fodder and borders are used for plantation of fragrant plants, medicinal herbs, *khus khus* etc.

- Apart from cropping patterns, Kautilya fixed minimum standard for grain yield and crop yield. He mentioned a number of cultivated crops and the conversion ratio of yield when de-husked or hulled. He also laid down standards of oil extraction yield, the spinning yield of cotton and the byproducts. He gave detailed account of cultivation after classifying the lands and average rainfall in certain regions.

➢ Harvesting

- Kautilya stated that "produce shall be collected immediately after harvesting. Nothing should be left in the field, not even chaff. Crops when reaped should be heaped up in high piles giving proper space. Threshing floor of different fields shall be situated close to each other".

B. Laborers and artisans

➢ Kautilya had a great compassion for workers; therefore, it was made mandatory for the landholders to arrange proper facilities for workers. They had to provide drinking water to the laborers on the threshing floor and other working places. He also warned the laborers not to bring any 'fire' (flammable items) on the threshing floor, to prevent fire incidents. He made arrangements to provide wages to workers and artisans in proportion to the amount of work done by them.

C. Rural development

➢ A village consists of not less than one hundred and not more than five hundred families of the cultivators. The village boundary shall be fixed upto one or two *krosa* (one *krosa*= 2 miles) which shall be denoted by a river or mountain, forest, trees, etc

➢ Land prepared for cultivation was given to tax payer only upto the life of the person. Lands were taken back from those who did not cultivate but gave to others for cultivation. The cultivators who regularly paid their taxes were entitled to get the supply of grain, cattle, money, etc

➢ Kautilya's Artha Shastra described the facilities given to spiritual guides, physicians, veterinary surgeon, horse trainers and messengers. Fertile land was given to skilled persons without tax but they did not have any right to sell or mortgage the land.

6.5 Our Journey in Agriculture

The settlements of Sindhu plains and Baluchistan hills revealed that agriculture began in India with barley and wheat cultivation along with goat and sheep herding. Such settlements expanded across Sindhu system from about 3500 BC and eventually to the plains. Thereafter, a wide agricultural settlement to the Southeast have arisen. Subsequent development in India relied on its secure agriculture base which produced Harappan culture. This culture assumed dominance and expanded agriculture.

A. The following are the main points in Indian journey in agriculture

- The Bhimbetka rock shelters are the archaeological site in Madhya Pradesh exhibiting the traces of human life on the Indian sub-continent
- Dog domestication by farmers occurred between 27,000 and 30,000 years ago
- The hymns of Rigveda and other vedic hymns on agriculture were divinely related to Rishis
- Around 12,000 years ago emmer wheat was domesticated
- Between 8000 and 6000 BC agriculture and animal husbandry developed in Indus–Saraswathi region and Vedas mention wooden plough, barley, interculture, harvesting, threshing, storage, animal management etc.
  - In the same period honey was valued for its taste and nutrition as well as being considered sacred
  - Barley was one of the first domesticated grains during the same period
- Between 6000 and 4000 BC Agastya Rishi was the first sage to cross Vindhya mountains southwards bringing north and south Indian agriculture together
  - Ramayana events occurred in the same period
  - In the same period Parasurama taught agriculture to farmers of Kerala
- Mahabharata events occurred around 4000 to 400 BC
- Mahabharata contains references to agriculture
- Charaka Samhita is an early text on Ayurveda

- Crude cane sugar was produced in India around 600 BC
- The first text book on agriculture "Krishiparashara" was compiled by sage Parashara
- Amarasimha compiled Amarakosha
- Kautilya wrote "Artha Shastra", an ancient Indian treatise
- The Sudarshan lake was constructed by Maurya rulers in 400 BC. The lake irrigated fields until 10th Century AD
- The grand anicut, built by Chola King Karikalan in 1st Century AD is one of the oldest water diversion or water regulator structures in the world on river Cauvery near Tiruchurapalli in Tamil Nadu
- Varahamihira wrote an encyclopedic work, "Brihat Samhita". It contained information on detecting ground water, methods of prediction of monsoon rainfall based on Astrology (Astronomy) which was accepted by the farmers
- Surapala compiled first ever complete text on arbori- horticulture in Sanskrit giving practices of "Vrikshurveda"
- Kashyapa wrote "Kashyapeya Krishisukthi" in which he gave detailed description of growing rice and listed 26 rice varieties with characteristics
- Raja Todaramal introduced land survey and revenue districts and relevance of revenue collection
- "Krishi Gita" was compiled and edited in 15 th Century AD by Vidvan Govinda Warriar. The text has information on soil and crop management
- Between 1900 and 1947 AD major changes taken place in farming systems, mechanization, plant and animal exploration, introduction of crops and animals in new areas
    - In the same period domination of European agriculture systems over ancient and indigenous methods occurred
    - With USA joining, the animal power was replaced with fuel power
    - Progress was made in developing chemical fertilizers
- After Indian independence in 1947 AD Indian agriculture made rapid progress in creating institutions and trained staff
- The first agricultural university was established in 1960 at Pantnagar (Uttarakhand)

- Country wide networks for research on crops and animals were established
- By 2000 AD Indian agricultural research gained prestigious status world wide

B. Some key Contributions made by Distinguished Agricultural Scientists

- M S Swaminathan: With tremendous intellectual input and exceptional vision, elevated the status of Indian agriculture to height at global level as "Father of Green revolution in India".
- B R Barwale : A noted philanthropist, started with a small seed business and took it to make a mark at global level and he pioneered seed business in india
- C T Patel : Successfully worked out a method to produce world's first cotton hybrid (1970) and his technology was adopted world wide
- A S Atwal : Developed the first commercial hybrid of pearlmillet (hybrid bajra No.1) which gave the double yields
- Y L Nene: Solved the mystery of Khaira disease of rice in tarai region of Uttarakhand. Founder – Chairman of Asian Agri History Foundation, the treasure of South and South East agricultural heritage
- Verghese Kurien : Social entrepreneur known as "Father of white revolution"
- B V Rao : Known as "Father of Indian poultry industry" he transformed poultry from a mere backyard activity into an organized world class industry
- MVK Siva Kumar: Known as "Father of modern agrometeorology" in the world, taken the operational agrometeorology to all the continents of the world.

6.6 Natural Resources

A. Weather and climate

- The key to successful agriculture is weather and climate, especially monsoon rainfall. Agriculture is largely weather and climate sensitive. Nearly 70 % of total cultivated land in India depends on rainfall for assured crop yield. Rain is an essential weather element for agriculture. It is the most precious gift of nature. There is no alternative and a primary requirement for agriculture

- Vagaries of weather and climate can neither be adjusted nor controlled
- However, scientists have been able to devise means of minimising some unfavourable effects by way of forecasting weather
- The ancient knowledge on weather forecasting is unique to Indian agriculture
- Even today village level meteorologists are right to high percentage of their weather prediction
- The most important and surprising aspect regarding ancient scriptures written by astrologers is that weather of coming year or even years together can be predicted with high percentage of accuracy, even before the start of the years
- The rules developed are simple and costly apparatus is not required
- Observation coupled with experience extending over centuries enabled the great sages of India to delve deep into the subject of meteorology and discover the laws governing weather which is of utmost importance to farmers
- A time has come to use both ancient and modern scientific knowledge and methods of weather forecasting for agriculture
- Weather is a non-monetary input in agriculture
- Weather- health must be maintained and weather based agriculture reap excellent harvests and benefits to farmers.

B. Soil

- Soil is next most valuable natural resource after weather that sustain the existence of agriculture
- India is endowed with considerable ecological diversity, large volume of tapped and untapped sources of water, abundant sunlight, and large animal and human populations. Indian liabilities, apart from those caused by population growth and aberrant weather, mostly arise from an improper use and management of the natural resources

- Soil is one of the basic requirements for agriculture. Inspite of modern technologies like hydroponics and aeroponics which are expensive ways to grow plants and which are feasible only under limited circumstances, most plant production for man's benefit will continue to use the soil as the source and substrata of plant growth
- The soil and weather constitute the very basis of agricultural, animal and forestry products. The highest importance has to be given to the conservation, development and utilization of these resources
- It is in the interest of present as well as future generations that soil health must be maintained. Some civilizations viewed the soil as sacred material which must be handed down to coming generations intact
- One of the major factors responsible for low crop yields is the growing loss of top fertile soil, causing damage to soil health and fertility. It is evident from the fact that "while it takes anywhere between one 100-400 years for one centimeter of top soil to be formed in nature, all this soil can be lost in just one year due to erosion."

C. Plant **(Genetic resources)**

- In no country in the world are grown as many crops and with as much genetic variability as in India. Some plants are introduced from the New World into India
- Considerable variability generated subsequent to their arrival in India. A few examples are maize, chilli, potato and cucurbits.

6.7 Green Revolution and its Impact and Concerns

Agriculture is an age old practice. Introduction of high yielding varieties of rice and wheat coupled with befitting management technologies and expansion in irrigation network gave birth to one of the most applauded success stories of post independent India- Green revolution.

The term "Green revolution" was coined by Dr. William Gaud of United States Department of Agriculture in 1968. The four major components of green revolution are

- technology- the prime mover of change
- services- which can take technology to farmers

- policies- to fix prices of inputs and outputs
- farmers enthusiasm

About 80 % of food production comes from farmers with small holdings. For them agriculture is the backbone of livelihood. Hence, higher productivity per unit of arable land and irrigation water is essential to produce profitable crops. This should, however, be achieved without harm to the ecological foundations essential for sustainable agriculture.

- ➢ History unveils that agriculture in totality, practiced in ancient times, produced healthy crops and livestock and the health of the society and weather and climate was also maintained
- ➢ However, natural resources such as weather, soil, plant material etc., are getting degraded due to modern developmental programmes which are executed without visualizing the disastrous consequences
- ➢ Even some real good programmes have been found causing havoc because of faulty planning and implementation with utter neglect of ancient and indigenous technologies which have stood the test of time
- ➢ In the race for modernization of agriculture, India have mortgaged all that was good in time-tested ancient and traditional technologies
- ➢ With the result, India is paying a very heavy price in terms of deteriorating weather and climate, soil and plant (genetic) resources
- ➢ So far as soil is concerned, its fertility is fast getting depleted; this is because of increasing cropping intensity involving heavy doses of chemical fertilizers, pesticides and soil amendments

In the most successful green revolution areas where wheat-rice rotation has become a great cropping system, the problems noticed are

- heavy dependence of fertilizers and decreasing percentage of restorative crops like legumes in the crop rotation
- increasing micro-nutrient deficiency
- decreasing efficiency of fertilizers
- greater depletion of aquifer and falling water table
- increased dependence on pesticides and disturbing natural equilibrium

- increased use of tractors and other heavy machinery, making agriculture a capital intensive industry and
- declining availability of forages and reduced emphasis on integration of crop and animal production system.

The situation underlines the need to improve weather health; integrated nutrient management; integrated pest management and genetic resource conversation systems.

Dr. M S Swaminathan played excellent role in Green revolution. In 1982, he said that the green revolution should become an "ever-green revolution" leading to enhancement of production without ecological harm. He also stated that in this era of climate change that small farmers are facing, there is urgent need for "ever green revolution".

The Ever- green revolution for small farmers relies on

- organic and green agricultural practices which include cultivation without the use of chemical inputs such as chemical fertilizers and pesticides
- conservation farming with the help of integrated pest management, integrated nutrient management and integrated natural resource management.

6.8 Sustainable Agriculture

Sustainability of agriculture is increasingly becoming a matter of serious concern worldwide. Sustainability basically refers to "An agricultural production system which meets the needs of growing population without degrading and depleting the natural resources".

- ➢ Sustainable agriculture does not mean that it can sustain ever-increasing population growth
- ➢ Among the major factors that determine crop or livestock productivity, weather, soil and plant (genetic) resources are the most crucial and vital ones
- ➢ However, these precious natural resources are fast getting depleted, degraded and degenerated because of growing population, industrialization, urbanisation and change in life styles

- Productive and sustainable agriculture calls for some policy decision to ensure
  - no use or less use of chemicals
  - no over exploitation or mining of ground water
  - no oversupply of water in canal irrigation commands
  - no erosion of endangered crops, seeds and breeds
  - no colossal wastage of rain water to the sea
  - in addition to the above, sustainable agriculture demands, to follow the traditional farming systems with a modern scientific perspective, even subordinating some interests for the sake of sustainable development.

6.9 Description by Travellers from Foreign Countries (China, Europe and USA)

There is evidence that most of the crops of importance were grown in regions of Asia around 9500-12000 years ago. Wide diversity of crops, soils, climates etc., have resulted in generation of a variety of ancient technical knowledge and feeding large human population. It is agricultural wealth and richness of India that prompted the European nations to come out of their cold climates in search of Indian green pastures, first as traders, then as colonizers and rulers.

- Mr.E.Buck frankly accepted before the Famine Commission of 1880 that "If foreigners try to dominate Indian farmer in one technology the Indian farmers dominate with hundred technologies"
- The Collector of Ratnagiri wrote: "The southern Konkan has nothing to learn from western countries or America in rice culture"
- Early researches in sericulture were made by W.M.H.Smith in 1814. Next year Mr.N.G.Mukherjee, a scholar, was commissioned by government for the investigation of silk-worm disease in Bengal. That year he submitted a note on the decline of silk trade in Bengal. He advised the Government to establish a sericultural laboratory

- In agricultural education Wellesley was the first Governor-General who talked of "model farms" and "farming" as a branch of agricultural instruction
- In 1860's the Landholder's Association and the British Indian Association repeatedly asked for education in agriculture
- Break was given by the Government of Madras in 1865 by establishing an experimental farm at Saidapet. Facilities for testing the merits of little known machines, implements, manures, crops, systems of culture, livestock, etc., were created. These efforts believed to be successful and the implements, manures etc., suited more or less to the requirements of southern India were propagated
- Saidapet farm superintendent, Mr. Robertson pointed out how literary education had robbed agriculture of her best men and called for the establishment of an agricultural college. He persisted and got an agricultural college opened at Saidapet in 1876
- Col.Wilks said "the practice of Indian farmer was built on the most enlightened principles of modern farming".

6.10 Vision for the Future- Challenges Ahead

The greatest challenge to human being today is becoming a good ancestor. The challenge can be met through a mass movement which can promise a healthy weather and climate and other natural resources to the generations yet to be born.

- More than hundred years ago Swami Vivekananda has said "so long as they forget the past, the nation remained in a state of dark and as soon as they have begun to look into their past, there is on every side a fresh manifestation of life. It is out of this past that the future has to be moulded, this past will become the future". He also said that "the more the Indians study the past, the more glorious will be their future, and who so ever tries to bring the past to the door of everyone, is a benefactor to the nation"
- Foreigners always emphasized that the "scientific" agriculture originated only in the Western countries and the Indian farming systems had always been "unscientific". Literature indicates that curricula in agriculture even today continue to reflect the Western

bias. The glorious past of Indian agriculture was never highlighted correctly. It is only during the past two decades that the West itself has recognized that many of their "scientific" practices led to unsustainable agriculture and only then the agricultural scientists of India turned their attention to the study of traditional and indigenous farming systems

- It is imperative that the agricultural scientists of India are thoroughly educated in traditional agriculture. Only then, there will be a meaningful interaction between farmers and scientists. This in turn should lead to sound agriculture progress towards sustained food security
- In Mao's words, "water supply is the thread of life of agriculture". India is fortunate that the average annual precipitation is the second largest in the world, next only to South America. Even if half of the rain water is properly conserved and used for irrigation, the entire arable land in India can produce two crops a year. But, most of the rainwater not only runs off to the sea and goes a total waste, but also, it erodes much of Indian good soil. The wastage of water flowing to the sea can be reduced considerably by keeping the land covered with forest, grasses and crops. The land which is densely covered facilitates seepage of more water into the soil and thereby augments ground water which can be later pumped up to irrigate the fields
- But, the land is getting degraded at an alarming rate because of reckless felling of forests and unregulated grazing of the grass lands, leading to more and more run off to water. The traditional tanks and ponds also drain into the sea which could otherwise be utilized for irrigation either directly or through recharge of ground water. What is, therefore, urgently needed is re-afforestation of exposed land and desilting of century old tanks and ponds wherever possible.

Several other measures as appropriate for the benefit of the farmers shall also be given top priority for sustainable climate smart agriculture and food security through better weather health.

Appendix

A tree forgives you like mother, even if you hit with a stone it gives a fruit

N
MEDIEVAL INDIA
TIBET
Jhelum
Chenab
Ravi
Satluj
Indus
KARNAL
Indraprastha
Ganga
Yamuna
Chatayala
Jodhpur
Varanasi
Patliputra
Monghyr
Brahmaputra
ASSAM
CHENDELLAS
Prayag
Nalanda
Partabgarh
Ujjain
PALAS
PARAMARAS
Narmada
Mahanadi
Tapti
Godavai
BAY
OF
BENGAL
KALINGA
RASHTRAKUTAS
ARABIAN
SEA
Krishna
Andaman and Nicobar Island
(INDIA)
CHOLAS
Kaveri
Lakshadweep Island
(INDIA)
CHERAS
PANDYAS
INDIAN OCEAN

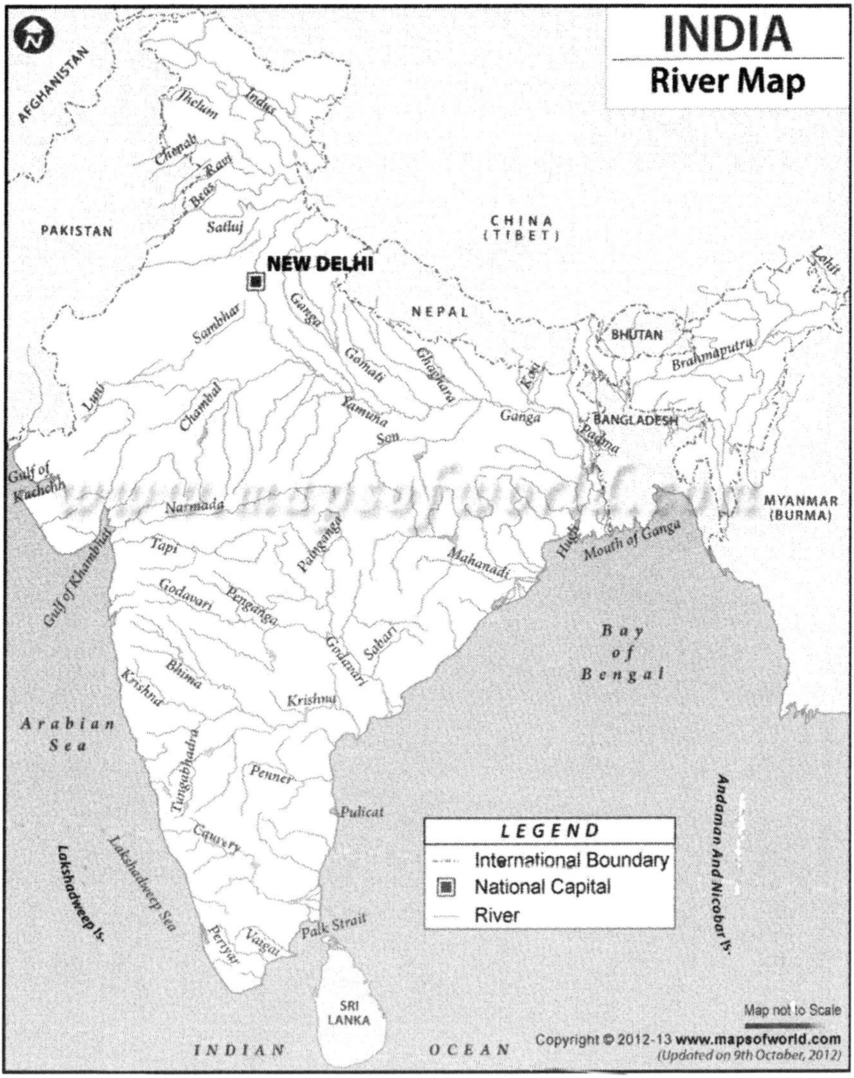
INDIA
River Map
AFGHANISTAN
PAKISTAN
CHINA (TIBET)
NEW DELHI
NEPAL
BHUTAN
BANGLADESH
MYANMAR (BURMA)
Jhelum
Indus
Chenab
Ravi
Beas
Satluj
Sambhar
Ganga
Gomati
Ghaghara
Kosi
Brahmaputra
Lohit
Luni
Chambal
Yamuna
Son
Padma
Gulf of Kachchh
Narmada
Tapi
Gulf of Khambhat
Penganga
Mahanadi
Hugli
Mouth of Ganga
Godavari
Sabari
Bhima
Krishna
Bay of Bengal
Arabian Sea
Tungabhadra
Penner
Pulicat
Cauvery
Lakshadweep Is.
Lakshadweep Sea
Periyar
Vaigai
Palk Strait
SRI LANKA
Andaman And Nicobar Is.
LEGEND
International Boundary
National Capital
River
Map not to Scale
INDIAN OCEAN
Copyright © 2012-13 www.mapsofworld.com
(Updated on 9th October, 2012)

References

1. Choudhary, S.L.,Saxena, R.C.and Nene, Y.L. (ed). 2006. Bridging Gap between Ancient and Modern Technologies to Increase Agricultural Productivity. Proceedings of the National Conference held from 16 to 18 December 2005. Central Arid Zone Research Institute, Jodhpur, Rajasthan Asian Agri-History Foundation (AAHF), Secunderabad; and Rajasthan Chapter of AAHF Udaipur 313002, Rajasthan, India.

2. Murthy, V.R.K. 2015: Climate change- Weather Health Indices as tools and services in Agriculture. The Andhra Agric.J. 62 (4): 737-745.

3. Murthy, V.R.K. 2016: Principles and practices of agricultural disaster management. Textbook. Book Syndicate Publishers, Koti, Hyderabad, Andhra Pradesh, India ISBN 978-93-83635-97-9 PP 243.

4. Nalini Sadhale (Tr) 1999. Krishi – Parashara (Agriculture by Parashara). Agri- Histroy Bulletin No. 2. Asian Agri – History foundation, Secundrabad, India.

5. Nalini Sadhale (Tr.). 1996. Surapala's Vrikshayurveda (The Science of Plant Life by Surapala). Agri- History Bulletin No.1 Asian Agri-History Foundation, Foundation, Secunderabad 500009, India.

6. Nalini Sadhale and Nene, Y.L. (ed). 2008. Mriga. Pakshi. Shastra (The Science of Animals and Birds). Asia Agri-History Foundation, Secunderabad 500009, India.

7. Nene, Y.L. and Choudhary, S.L. 2002. Agricultural heritage of India. Asian Agri – History foundation, Secundrabad.

8. Nene, Y.L. and Choudhary,S.L.(ed). 2002. Agricultural Heritage of India. Proceedings of the National Conference held from 10 to 13 February 2002. Rajasthan College of Agriculture, Udaipur,

Rajasthan. Asian Agri- History Foundation (AAHF), Secunderabad; and Rajasthan Chapter of AAHF, Udaipur 313002, Rajasthan, India.

9. Nene, Y.L.(ed). 2007. Glimpses of the Agricultural heritage of India. Asian Agri-History Foundation, Secunderabad 500009, India.
10. Randhawa, M.S. 1980 – 86. A histroy of Agriculture in India.Vol.I, II, III and IV. Indian council of Agricultural Research, New Delhi.
11. Raychaudhuri, S.P. 1964. Agriculture in ancient India. Indian council of Agricultural Research, New Delhi.
12. Razia Akbar (Tr) 2000. Muskha Dar Fauni – Falahat (The art of agriculture). Agri – History Bulletin No. 3. Asian Agri. History foundation, Secundrabad.
13. Saxena, R.C., Choudhary, S.N and Nene, Y.L. 2009. A text book on Ancient History of Indian Agriculture. Asian Agri- History Foundation (AAHF) Secunderabad 50009. And Rajasthan Chapter of AAHF, Udaipur 313002, India.
14. Sivakumar, M.V.K. 2017: Invited article on "Impacts of climate change on agriculture" The Andhra Agric.J. 63(4): 1-5.